ROCKBOUND

ROCKBOUND

Written and Composed by Allen Cole
Based on the Novel by Frank Parker Day

Rockbound
first published 2011 by
Scirocco Drama
An imprint of J. Gordon Shillingford Publishing Inc.

Scirocco Drama Editor: Glenda MacFarlane
Cover design by Terry Gallagher/Doowah Design Inc.
Cover art by Jyelle Vogel
Author photo by David Cooper
Printed and bound in Canada on 100% post-consumer recycled paper.

We acknowledge the financial support of the Manitoba Arts Council and The Canada Council for the Arts for our publishing program.

Production inquiries should be addressed to:
Allen Cole
a.cole@rogers.com

Library and Archives Canada Cataloguing in Publication

Cole, Allen
Rockbound / Allen Cole.—1st ed.

A musical, adapted from the novel by Frank Parker Day.
ISBN 978-1-897289-61-7

1. Musicals—Librettos. I. Title.

ML50.C689R68 2011 782.1′40268 C2011-901116-6

J. Gordon Shillingford Publishing
P.O. Box 86, RPO Corydon Avenue, Winnipeg, MB Canada R3M 3S3

Thank you to Jean Travers.

Characters

Uriah Jung: ....Patriarch of Rockbound

David Jung: ....Uriah's second cousin and sharesman

Casper Jung:..................Uriah's eldest son

Joseph Jung: ....Uriah's youngest son

Tamar Jung:...................Uriah's eldest daughter

Ruth Jung:.......................Uriah's youngest daughter

Alma Jung: ....Joseph's wife

Simeon Jung:.................Uriah's older brother

Gershom Born:..............Uriah's sharesman, singer, storyteller

Old Gershom Born:......Keeper of the Barren Island Light, Gershom's father

Fanny: ....potato-girl, works for the Jungs

Anapest Kraus: ....Empress of the Krauses, Uriah's cousin

Christian Kraus:............Anapest's eldest son

Melcher Kraus: ....Anapest's youngest son

Mary Dauphiny:...........Rockbound schoolteacher

Rollie Dauphiny: ....Mary's fisherman father

Voice of the Barren Island Lighthouse, Voice of the Black and Yellow Dog, Various Residents of Sanford

Notes

Rockbound is written and composed to be performed by seven male actors, four female actors, an accordion player, a bass player and a drummer.

Text which is to be sung is printed in **bold**.

Scene 18: Graveyard

EXYOU is in Bosnia. He enters a graveyard carrying a gravestone. He has a camera around his neck. An OLD WOMAN lays flowers on a grave. EXYOU looks for the grave of his son and wife.

EXYOU: Sorry to disturb you but I am looking for the grave of my wife and child. I was told from the forensic centre that they were buried under the oak tree but I can't find it anywhere.

OLD WOMAN: Obviously, someone who is still alive chopped that tree for firewood.

EXYOU: Someone's keeping warm with a graveyard tree in their stove?

OLD WOMAN: People warm up in different ways. Last winter someone chopped out every single wooden cross. You should be thankful gravestones don't burn. Where are you coming from?

EXYOU: Canada.

OLD WOMAN: Ah, he returns. A camera around his neck like a true tourist.

EXYOU: I was a photojournalist. I documented the war.

OLD WOMAN: If they were recently moved from the NN section they'd be around here.

EXYOU: What is this NN section?

OLD WOMAN: It stands for "No Name". People whose identity is unknown. Once the Forensic Center is able to recognize them, then they move the bones to this section. Your family must be somewhere here now.

EXYOU is reading the name engraved on a gravestone.

EXYOU: Petrovich? Miro Petrovich? What is he doing here?

OLD WOMAN: He's resting in peace.

EXYOU: Don't you know who that is? Miro "the Ubica." *(Translation: the killer.)* He's that sniper that shot at the bus full of evacuating orphans. I can't place my wife and child's gravestone here. They shouldn't be buried beside him.

OLD WOMAN: They're both victims of the same war.

EXYOU: My wife and child wouldn't be victims if it wasn't for people like him.

OLD WOMAN: I wish he could've watched the war through the lens of a camera, like you, instead of the lens of a gun. He played the piano beautifully. After the war he surrendered. I tried my best to comfort him, I didn't know he was already dead inside, last month he killed himself. Please, let's imagine the oak tree was here. Let me help you with that gravestone.

EXYOU says the names of his wife and child as he lays down the stone…

EXYOU: Dushan…Mata…

Allen Cole

Originally from Nova Scotia, Allen Cole has worked variously as composer, lyricist and / or book writer on musicals such as *The Wrong Son*, *The Bricklin* (with Paul Ledoux), *Anything That Moves* (with Ann-Marie MacDonald and Alisa Palmer), and *Pélagie* (with Vincent de Tourdonnet). He has won numerous awards, including four Dora Mavor Moore Awards, and a Best Film Score Award from the Atlantic Film Festival. In 2009, *Rockbound* won five Merritt Awards, including Best New Play, Best Music and Best Production. *Rockbound* was also shortlisted for the prestigious Lieutenant-Governor of Nova Scotia Masterworks Award.

Scene 19: Ghosts

ALEJANDRA: Taxi!

EXYOU: Where to?

ALEJANDRA: To the lake. You know that little peninsula west of Sunnyside?

EXYOU: Yes, I know it.

ALEJANDRA notices the Polaroids covering the interior of the taxi.

ALEJANDRA: Are you a photographer?

EXYOU: Yes, I am still a photographer, despite predictions to the contrary.

ALEJANDRA: I am a writer who doesn't write anymore… I've never been in a cab like this with so many stories, silences hanging from the walls.

EXYOU: Ghosts.

ALEJANDRA: Ghosts! You collect ghosts!

EXYOU: Ghosts of their former selves.

ALEJANDRA: Right.

He looks up at her through the mirror. Long pause. They arrive.

EXYOU: Well, here we are.

ALEJANDRA: It is so peaceful.

ALEJANDRA pays and exits the cab.

EXYOU: Wait! Can I take your picture?

ALEJANDRA: You can, but I'm already a ghost.

EXYOU: No. You are not a ghost.

ALEJANDRA: Sure, hang my picture.

EXYOU takes ALEJANDRA's picture.

Scene 20: Award Ceremony

SEEYYEE is at a large auditorium receiving an award.

EMCEE: Ladies and Gentlemen. We are honouring a very special woman this evening. She spent ten years imprisoned for fighting for equal rights for the Oromo People in Ethiopia who were persecuted for their ethnicity. She was forced into exile and sought refuge in Canada. Tonight we honour Seeyyee Sera.

SEEYYEE: Thank you very much. *(She looks at her notes.)* I am very honoured to be… *(A long pause.)* I had a speech prepared but…I'd like to ask my baby brother to be with me here tonight.

She lights a candle.

The last time I heard my brother's voice, I was crying into the phone. I could see the turbulent billows of smoke rise over my homeland. I could see the fire spread and the flames dance all around him. Agitated tongues of flame lashed out to lick my brother. Yet, he stood there smiling, so sure.

We hear drums.

BABY BROTHER: Stay put my big sister, stay put. I'm home; you are the one in exile. Stay put till you come home to freedom.

SEEYYEE: But, what is home and what is exile? Oh, I enjoy home in exile, when you are rendered homeless at home.

In my homeland, Baby Brother, in my homeland,
The grass shades me from the scorching sun;
but in exile, Baby Brother,
the sun burns me in the thickest shade of the biggest tree.
In my homeland, Baby Brother, in my homeland
The meat of a flea feeds a multitude;
but in exile, Baby Brother,
Two friends fight over the meat of an elephant.

BABY BROTHER: Home is freedom, my big sister, home is bilisummaa. *(Translation: Freedom.).* Home is dignity. Home is justice. Exile is wherever home is not.

SEEYYEE: Exile is wherever they plough the fields with guns and sow the seeds with blood. In an unjust world, home can only be in the struggle to restore freedom and justice.

BABY BROTHER: Yes, that's why I took to the woods with the village youth.

SEEYYEE: Our father took to the woods, and I am not coming home
Our father's brother took to the woods, and I am not coming home
Our mother's brother took to the woods, and I am not coming home
I saw the injustice
And my heart howls.
Oh my heart howls with rage.

Drums stop. SEEYYEE is back in reality.

SEEYYEE: *(To the audience.)* Thank you.

Scene 21: Ashes

XIAO HONG enters the taxi. She holds her mother's ashes in an urn.

EXYOU: Hello. It's been a while. You have no luggage?

XIAO HONG: No. I haven't traveled in a long time. I just came to pick up my mother. We'd like to go to the lake please. *(Talking to the urn.)* We are making a left turn now. You will soon see the city of Toronto where I have made my home. Ma, we are crossing a bridge now. Do you remember that picture I took with the sunset? It was here. We are exiting an off-ramp. There is the beautiful Lake Ontario up ahead. I wrote to you so many times about it. You said in your letter that you wanted to see it one day.

EXYOU: Many people can't say goodbye when they are alive but meet again in another world.

XIAO HONG: My mother's final wish was that she be reunited with me. Her remains were smuggled out of the country and a good friend sent them to me. The spirits of the dead do not recognize the routes in the human world; and so I must talk to her at each point and at each turn so she will not lose her way. She grew up by a river. She always loved the water.

EXYOU: I know a beautiful tree on the north shore. Here we are.

XIAO HONG arrives at Lake Ontario's shore, clutching the urn.

XIAO HONG: Ma, we are here now, in our new home.

She ritualistically removes the contents. She scatters the ashes into the water.

The End.

Act II

Scene 1: 17. *Community Meeting*: Fanny, Uriah, Anapest, Casper

18. *Ralph*: David, Ensemble

19. *Mary's Entrance*: Male Ensemble

Scene 2: No songs

Scene 3: 20. *Jane an' de Li'l Bird*: Mary

21. *Orion/She Don't Know*: Mary, David, Ensemble

Scene 4: No songs

Scene 5: 22. *De Louise*: Casper

23. *Come Fog or Snow*: Gershom

24. *We'll Be Married in de Spring*: Gershom, Mary

Scene 6: 25. *Act II, Sc. 6 underscore*: Ensemble

Scene 7: 26. *A Pretty Kettle o' Fish* (reprise 2): Uriah, Gershom, Ensemble

Scene 8: 27. *Ole Dukie's Boat*: Casper, Gershom

28. *De Bull*: Gershom, Ensemble

Scene 9: 29. *When I Grow Old* (reprise): Gershom, David, Ensemble

Scene 10: 30. *Act II Finale*: David, Mary, Ensemble

List of Songs

Act I

Scene 1: 1. *Old Gershom's Advice*: Old Gershom, Ensemble

Scene 2: 2. *A Pretty Kettle o' Fish*: David, Uriah, Joseph, Casper, Ensemble

3. *No Light*: David, Ensemble

Scene 3: 4. *Fish House Groove*: Uriah, Ensemble

5. *Why's Tomorrow Got To Be Sunday*: Uriah, Ensemble

6. *When I Grow Old*: Gershom

7. *In de Sweet By an' By*: Fanny, Ensemble

Scene 4: 8. *The Barren Island Light*: Gershom, Ensemble

9. *David's Prayer*: David, Ensemble

Scene 5: 10. *He's a Smart Lad*: Tamar, Uriah, Ensemble

Scene 6: 11. *The Barren Island Light* (reprise): Gershom, Ensemble

Scene 7: 12. *A Pretty Kettle o' Fish* (reprise): David, Uriah, Ensemble

Scene 8: 13. *Seben Crows*: Gershom

14. *The Story of the Sanford Ghos'*: Gershom, David, Ensemble

15. *Seben Crows* (reprise): Gershom

Scene 9: 16. *Act I Finale*: David, Tamar, Ensemble

Production History

Rockbound was first produced by Two Planks and a Passion Theatre and premiered in Canning, Nova Scotia, in July, 2009. This production also toured to Chester Playhouse in Chester, NS, with the following cast:

DAVID Jung .... James MacDonald

URIAH Jung .... Frank Moore

CASPER Jung .... Kyle Gillis

TAMAR / ALMA Jung .... Bridget Bezanson

JOSEPH Jung .... Leete Stetson

RUTH Jung / MARY Dauphiny .... Amanda LeBlanc

SIMEON Jung / OLD GERSHOM / ROLLIE .... Cliff LeJeune

GERSHOM Born / MELCHER Kraus .... Marty Burt

FANNY .... Margot Sampson

ANAPEST Kraus .... Burgandy Code

CHRISTIAN Kraus / JOHNNY Publicover .... Ryan Rogerson

Percussion: Mark Adam, Bass: Chris Churchill, Accordion and Glockenspiel: Sandy Moore

Directed by Ken Schwartz

Set Design by Ken Schwartz

Costume Design by Rosie Browning

Musical Direction by Allen Cole

Choreography by Alexis Milligan

Stage Manager: Marisa West

Apprentice Stage Manager: Austin Cole

Property Manager: Michael McMahon

Act I

Scene 1

Duren Bay, early evening. DAVID JUNG is rowing vigourously in his yellow dory. He's a young man, around twenty. He rows with the confidence of a man who has spent his life on the water. DAVID has just left his home on the island of Big Outpost, and he's headed, with great determination, toward another island...Rockbound. At the moment, in the darkness, neither island can be seen. DAVID appears to be a yellow speck in the middle of a vast expanse of blue ocean. Stars glimmer in the sky.

Suddenly a beam of light makes a circular sweep through his path...the light from the distant Barren Island lighthouse. OLD GERSHOM appears as DAVID rows. OLD GERSHOM takes occasional sips from a jug of rum.

OLD GERSHOM: **One tent' o' de island o' Rockbound is yours, boy**
Yours by law, yours by law
Come to ye t'rough yur grandfader
Edward Jung, Ole Edward Jung

Yur Uncle Uriah
Dat ole miser
He's a shifty talkin' bugger
He's gonna try to tell ye different
Don't let 'im, don't let 'im!

If ye has to

Climb in yur boat an' go to Liscomb

Have a talk wid lawyer Kingsford

Claim yur right, David

Claim yur right

Ye t'ink I'se nuttin' but de foolish ole lighthouse keeper?

Don't know what I'se talkin'?

Well I been writin' de deeds, de wills an' de mortgages 'roun' here

Fur forty year

Forty year, David

I knows

One tent' o' de island o' Rockbound is yours, boy

Yours by law, yours by law

Come to ye t'rough yur grandfader

Edward Jung, Ole Edward Jung

The light from the lighthouse sweeps over DAVID again. OLD GERSHOM disappears. DAVID continues rowing, approaches Rockbound, ties his dory to a spike, and jumps ashore.

Scene 2

Rockbound. As DAVID ties his dory and climbs ashore, URIAH Jung approaches. URIAH is a strong man of seventy. He is intimidating in his yellow oilskins, which are spotted with blood and sequins of herring scales. He eyes DAVID with distrust.

URIAH: An' what might ye be wantin'?

DAVID: I wants fur to be yur sharesman.

URIAH: **Scrawny whelp like you cain't ketch nuttin'?**
No p'int, is it?
No p'int a'tall
I'se seed ye afore, out de Outposts
Don't t'ink I haven't!
Us works here on Rockbound
Us has half a day's work done
'Fore youse Outposters rub de sleep out o' yur eyes
Ain't it!

URIAH gestures to CASPER, his eldest son. CASPER approaches.

Ain't dis a pretty kettle o' fish?
De pup wants to be my sharesman
Ain't dis a pretty kettle o' fish?
Wouldn't know a codfish
If de damn t'ing bit 'im!

URIAH and CASPER laugh.

CASPER: **Where's his gear?**
Where's his clothes?

URIAH: **Queer tramp like him ain't got nuttin'**

CASPER: **Jus' his nekkid feets**

URIAH: **An' a li'l yaller dory**

CASPER: **An' he prob'ly stole dat too, I lays**

URIAH: **Prob'ly try to steal one o' my boats too**

CASPER: **Prob'ly try to steal yur Lettie**

If ye turns yur back

JOSEPH, URIAH's youngest son, comes to see what's going on.

URIAH: **Ain't dis a pretty kettle o' fish?**

De t'ief wants to be my sharesman

Ain't dis a pretty kettle o' fish?

Wouldn't know a lobster

If it pinched 'im in de arse!

JOSEPH: **No one'll take in a wharf rat like you**

CASPER: **Us ain't got nuttin' here fur puppies**

URIAH: **Don't be messin' aroun' wid Uriah**

JOSEPH: **Dey's no work fur girlish babies**

CASPER: **Bes' be doin' what Fader tells ye**

URIAH: **I'se de master o' dis here island**

An' I'se tellin' ye to git!

They turn to go. DAVID summons up his courage, steps forward.

DAVID: **I ain't no tramp, sir**

An' I ain't no wharf rat neider

An' as fur yon dory

I salvaged her from de sea

An' beat de man

What tried to steal 'er from me

An' I'd do de same to you, sir

Eben if you is my uncle

URIAH and his boys stop suddenly and turn around.

URIAH: What's dat you say?

DAVID: I owns one tent' o' dis island o' Rockbound t'rough my grandfader, ole Edward Jung, yur cousin what died twenny year ago. I knows it to be true 'cause Ole Gershom Born, Keeper o' de Barren Island Light, tole me back at de Outposts.

CASPER: If he's been talkin' to Ole Gershom Born, Fader, maybe dey's some sense to'—

URIAH: Shut yur mout', Casper. *(Pause. URIAH thinks.)* Ye mus' be David, Hazel's gaffer. Yur kin's all bin' dead fur ten year.

DAVID: Twelve year.

URIAH: *(Pause.)* What ye do wid de land?

DAVID: Live on it, grow timothy and cabbages, same as youse. An' I'se'll set up in de house on de hill.

CASPER: Dat's where we store de lobster pots!

DAVID: It's de house where me mudder died, an' it belongs to me.

JOSEPH: Ye ain't got no right.

DAVID: I'se got de same rights as Anapest an' de Krauses.

URIAH: Maybe you is got some rights, maybe you isn't, but ye cain't be no sharesman wid me.

DAVID: Den I'se'll squat on me land an' live in me house an' fish offshore in me dory.

CASPER: Wid nair a line or net to git bait?

DAVID: I got a line an' I kin pick up squid an' caplin on de beach.

URIAH: An' where will ye land yur boat? Ain't figurin' on usin' my launch, is ye?

DAVID: I kin land on de sand beach in Sou'west Cove an' haul me dory out.

JOSEPH: One summer storm'll make kindlin' wood o' yur dory.

DAVID: Den I'se'll land on Anapest's launch.

URIAH: Anapest!

DAVID: She's me aunt, ain't she?

URIAH: She's a Kraus!

DAVID: Anyhow, yur sharesman or no, I sticks and stays.

URIAH: I wouldn't never take ye fur no sharesman, 'cause ye couldn't hold up yur end wid my boys.

JOSEPH: Dat's right.

DAVID: Give me a fortnight's trial. If I cain't ketch fish fur fish an' haul net fur net wid dese two puffins, den I'se'll go back to de Outposts, no wages asked fur.

JOSEPH: He mus' be dreamin', Fader, t'inkin' we'd take on a sickly bugger de likes o' him!

CASPER: Skinny li'l runt t'inks he kin—

URIAH: Hold on! *(Pause.)* No wages, ye say?

DAVID: Dat's what I said.

URIAH: Deal! Haul yur dory on de launch. Ye'll be takin' *Phoebe* out tomorrow.

JOSEPH: Fader!

URIAH: She's stood idle since Mark drowned anyways.

CASPER: He ain't gonna be nuttin' but trouble, I tells ye!

URIAH: Worry not, boys. A mont' hence, he'll be beggin' to go back to de Outposts, jus' you wait!

URIAH, JOSEPH and CASPER exit. DAVID hauls his dory up on the launch and looks up the hill toward his mother's house.

DAVID: **Now I'se got a li'l house on de hill**
So's in de winter I kin keep away de chill
An' in de summer I kin listen to de rain
When it comes fallin' sof'ly on my winderpane

Yes, I'se got a li'l house on de hill
An' ye kin bet I'se'll git me a still
An' my rum'll be one hunderd twenny proof
An' I'se'll drink it underneat' my own roof

'Cause dat my moon dat shines down on de sea
I doesn't like it lookin' down on me
When I'se drinkin' an' carousin' t'rough de night
I doesn't want to see no light
No, when I'se lyin' wid a gal in de night
I doesn't want to see no light

Fader, I'se come back
To de island o' yur fader

An' his fader 'fore dat
To de island where ye raised me
To de island where ye died

Mudder, I'se come back
An' I done de wery t'ing
Dat I neber t'ought I could

I stood up to Ole Uriah
Wid my eyes open wide

Now I'se got a li'l house on de hill
An' fur my mudder I'se'll plant a dafferdil
An' fur my uncle I'se'll plant a stand o' cedars
So's I don't has to see dat gang o' crooks and cheaters

Now in de ebenin' when I needs a li'l heat
I'se got a sack fur to wrap 'roun' my feet
An' when I lay my body down in my bed
I'se got anoder sack to wrap 'round my head

'Cause dat my moon dat shines down on de sea
I doesn't like it glarin' down on me
When I'se sleepin' in de black o' de night
I doesn't want to see no light
No, when I'se sleepin' in de black o' de night
I doesn't want to see no light

ANAPEST enters with her sons, CHRISTIAN and MELCHER.

ANAPEST: What you doin' here?

DAVID: Ebenin', Aunt Anapest. I'se yur nephew David Jung from de Outposts.

ANAPEST: Know dat. What you doin' here, I said.

DAVID: Uriah's new sharesman.

ANAPEST: Ury's sharesman? Dat hellion'll work ye to de bone.

CHRISTIAN: Got an eye like a stinkin' eel, he does.

MELCHER: Durn right.

CHRISTIAN: An' ye won't git nuttin' fur yur summer's work when Joe an' Casper has figured expenses.

DAVID: Beginnin' I'se'll take what dey gives me. Some day, I'se'll take what I wants. I don't expect no mercy, Aunt Anapest, but I… Well, I hates to say, but I'se real—

ANAPEST reaches into her pocket, pulls out a hunk of bread, tosses it to DAVID.

ANAPEST: Stop talkin' an' eat dis. Brung it fur ye. Arter all, yur me brudder's son, if ye is Ury's sharesman.

CHRISTIAN: But Mudder, he's a Jung!

MELCHER: Papa always said, 'Don't have naught to do wid dem Jungs!"

ANAPEST: Well yur fader married a Jung, didn't he?

CHRISTIAN & MELCHER: Ay, but—

ANAPEST: Ay, but nuttin.

DAVID: I'se sorry to beg, but I'se'll pay when I gits me first mont's share. I'se got naught, but ye'll lose naught t'rough me.

CHRISTIAN: Why don't ye beg yur bread off Ury?

DAVID: He's too damn hard.

MELCHER: If ye cain't feed yurself, ye won't neber stay on Rockbound. Ain't dat right, Christian?

DAVID: I stays, I sticks, if I has to dig up de roots o' de field, if I has to eat gnarly mussels, boiled periwinkles an' an odd checkerback! An' I'se settin' up in me mudder's house on de hill.

CHRISTIAN: Dey's haunts dere, what'll twitch de clothes off ye nights, ain't it?

MELCHER: Durn right dey is.

ANAPEST: Christian, Melcher!

DAVID: I ain't skeered o' no haunts. On de Outposts I lived nex' house to de ghos' ketcher.

MELCHER: Ye mean...Johnny Publicover?

DAVID: Ay, Johnny Publicover, de same what ketched de fierce Sanford Ghos'.

CHRISTIAN: Ghos' or no, ye'll have a hard go here wid no bread.

ANAPEST: What ye talkin' so fur, ye great lump, to yur own cousin? Has his house an' land done ye air a good? Ain't Ury gittin' free grass an' cabbages off dat land fur dese ten year?

DAVID: Twelve year.

ANAPEST: Bread ye'll have, boy; t'ree big loaves a week if ye kin live on dat.

DAVID: Dat I kin, an' my t'anks to ye.

ANAPEST: Alright, den. Git to sleep, now. Ury's up an' off 'fore de sun rises!

ANAPEST, CHRISTIAN and MELCHER exit.

DAVID: Ye'll find me in de years to come no grudgin' neighbour, Aunt Anapest.

Scene 3

URIAH's fish house. One month later. URIAH, his family and sharesmen are all working hard, gibbing herring. The group includes: URIAH, SIMEON, JOSEPH, CASPER, DAVID, GERSHOM, TAMAR, RUTH and FANNY. They all wear oilskins spattered with herring blood and sou'westers, and their vocal rhythm ebbs and flows as they gib.

URIAH: **Dese fish here**
Dey ain't de fish we was ketchin' in de spring-time
Dem fish we was ketchin' in de spring-time
Dey was all she-fish, she-fish

DAVID enters with a basket of salt.

Quick, David, look alive, look alive
More salt ober dere, look alive, look alive, boy!

DAVID gives the salt to CASPER.

Dese fish here
Now dey's mos'ly he-fish
Dey's all full o' milt
All full o' milt
Take a look at dat dere

No-one looks.

I SAID DEY's ALL FULL O' MILT
TAKE A LOOK AT DAT DERE!

ALL: **Holy liftin', dey's all full o' milt!**

URIAH: **Hey boy**
Run out to de woodshed
An' git me another puncheon
Dis one's full to de brim

Dat's right, hurry up, hurry up, now, boy!

DAVID carries away URIAH's full puncheon, brings him an empty one.

My body's pretty good
But my legs is gone
Cain't git aroun' much
But I kin still split a fish
Wid de youngest and de strongest o' ye
Yuh, yuh, yuh,
Yuh, yuh, yuh, yuh
Still got my hands, ain't I?
Dat's right
Ye best look lively
'Cause I still got my hands!

David, ye lazy bugger
More salt fur de gals
More salt, more salt fur de gals!

CASPER: **Dat's right, boy**
More salt fur de gals, more salt fur de gals!

URIAH: **Casper?**
Shut up yur big mouth
Put on yur damn boots
Git off yur fat arse
An' bring some more fish!

CASPER: **But?**

URIAH: **Go!**

CASPER exits to get more fish. DAVID fetches

some salt for FANNY, TAMAR and RUTH, who laugh as he passes.

When me an' Simeon was only jus' young fellers

ALL: **Uhhh?**

URIAH: **We split close to eighty odd barrels once**
Member dat, Sim? Member dat?
Started in splittin' 'round t'ree in de afternoon
Kep' on splittin' 'til sundown nex' day
Neber took a res'
Neber took a res'
Did we Sim?

Gershom!

GERSHOM: **What?**

URIAH: **Stop talkin' to de gals**
An' git splittin'!

Me an' Simeon we neber eben stirred nor eat
'Cept ebery now and den
When de women folk came to poke
A tough ole crus' o' bread into our moufs
While we kep' splittin' an' a-splittin'
An' a-pullin' out guts
Rippin' out milt
Neber took a res'
Neber took a res'!
No, no, no

An' look at dis here crew

Auk-de-leba
Dey's a-huffin' an' a-puffin'
An' complainin' 'bout dis
Worryin' 'bout dat
Cain't eben gib fifty barrels
'Fore midnight!

Ain't no men knows how to work now'days

Ain't it, Simeon?

Simeon?

SIMEON is in his own world, gibbing feebly and drooling.

Ain't it?

URIAH kicks him.

SIMEON: **Ay, dat it is, dat it is, dat it is, Ury!**

URIAH: 'Member dat time we went down Liscomb, Sim? Run into dat queer sickly feller. T'ink he'd had de infantile paralysis. *(URIAH laughs.)* Bugger wanted a nickel, jus' 'cause his legs was…

CASPER enters with a huge wheelbarrow full of herring.

CASPER: Here it be, here it be. Stick in yur knife an' rip 'er out agin'. More work fur de women an' de feeble ole' men!

CASPER dumps out his wheelbarrow.

RUTH: Good Lord, dey's more?

TAMAR: Still a couple wheelbarrows full waitin' out back I lays.

JOSEPH: Us ain't neber seen 'em runnin' t'ick as dey was today.

CASPER: Mus' be de tides.

URIAH: Alright, youse. No time to was'e. Only five hours 'til midnight.

TAMAR: Us's workin' 'til midnight?

URIAH: Got to split all we kin 'fore de Sabbath, Tamar. Not me nor me brudder nor me fader nor his fader 'fore dat ain't neber worked on de Lord's Day.

GERSHOM: Damn shame, ain't it? All o' dem fine herrin' out in de bay, jus' a-waitin' on ye. Ain't ye tempted, Ury? Jus' dis once?

URIAH: Us ain't neber eber worked on de Lord's Day, I said! Dey's some t'ings more important dan fishin'.

GERSHOM: You'se talkin' 'bout gals?

URIAH: No, Gershom.

GERSHOM: Oh, you'se talkin' 'bout rum!

URIAH: I'se talkin' 'bout respectin' our Lord! Dat's what us does 'roun' here. Ain't it, Simeon? Simeon!

URIAH kicks SIMEON.

SIMEON: Ay, dat's a fac', Ury. Dat's a fac', dat's a fac'.

URIAH: Now git back to work, Gershom, 'fore I gives ye a cobbin'! Dat goes fur all o' ye!

The group sings and splits. URIAH reflects privately.

Why's tomorrow gotta be Sunday, Lord

Wid all o' dem herrin' still so near?

If we went out tomorrow, reckon in one day, Lord
I could more'n double what I caught all year

My boys is young an' rugged an' wiry, Lord
Dey don't need to res' fur a whole darn day
Why's tomorrow gotta be Sunday, Lord
Wid all o' dem herrin' swimmin' 'roun' an' 'roun'
An' 'roun' an' 'roun' de bay?

Did ye see 'em out dere, Lord?
Dey was millions of 'em
Jus' a-dartin' to an' fro

I could reach right down wid my hand
An' grab 'em, Lord
Dey's runnin' t'ick as hapjack dough

But Monday mornin' I'se afeard
I'se'll be cryin' out:
Where'd de li'l bastards go?

Why's tomorrow gotta be Sunday?

Reckon you owes me a big ole jewel, Lord
A big ole jewel in my crown
Fur givin' dese lazy buggers a whole day off, now, Lord
Wid all o' dem herrin' swimmin' 'roun' an' 'roun'
An' 'roun' an' 'roun' an' 'roun'

Neber seen 'em so'

Dartin' to an' fro'

T'ick as hapjack dough?

Neber, eber seen 'em so

T'ick

URIAH: Quick now, all o' youse, pick up de pace. David, git some more salt fur Joseph. Look alive, boy, we ain't got all night!

JOSEPH: Dat's right, Davy. An' fill 'er up good!

DAVID grabs a bushel basket full of salt, turns to bring it to JOSEPH.

I said fill 'er up good, boy. Didn't ye hear me? Dere's room fur lots more in dat basket, ye lazy bugger!

DAVID adds a little more salt, filling the basket to the top. JOSEPH sneaks up behind him. DAVID turns with the basket and trips over JOSEPH's foot, spilling the salt. TAMAR, RUTH and FANNY laugh along with JOSEPH.

URIAH: Alright, David, stop showin' off fur de lasses. Did ye come here to work, or didn't ye?

DAVID brushes himself off, ignores URIAH, and continues gibbing.

GERSHOM: Who brung in de mos' fish las' mont'? Dis young feller, ain't it?

CASPER: He's been darn lucky, I'se'll give him dat.

DAVID: Ain't luck!

GERSHOM: Already caught more'n you'll catch in half a year, Casper.

TAMAR: Dat mean he's stickin', Fader?

URIAH: Seems dese sons o' mine can't keep up wid dis

skinny runt from de Outposts. So looks like he sticks.

DAVID: I ain't from de Outposts. I'se from dis here island.

FANNY: Where'er he comes from, he's a pretty feller.

GERSHOM: Prettier'n me, Fanny?

FANNY: Ye know you'se my favourite, Gershom.

JOSEPH: Ye'd best stick to yur taters, Fanny. Eber since ye got here, ye're runnin' roun' wid ebery man on Rockbound. Dey's a word fur a girl like dat.

TAMAR: Don't listen, Fanny. Joseph's jus' jealous 'cause ye neber run roun' wid him.

RUTH: But ye bes' be careful, Fanny. Mudder used to say, 'A lil' o' dat's all right maybe when you'se young, but if ye keeps on you'se'll neber git a man?'

FANNY: Us was made fur de good o' mens, an' mens was made fur de good of us, dat's what I says.

GERSHOM: An' I says de same. *(He and FANNY laugh.)*

TAMAR: What do ye t'ink, David? Is us womens made fur de good o' mens?

Embarassed, DAVID keeps working, says nothing.

FANNY: An' is you made fur de good o' womens, Davy? Davy? I bet you is, I jus' bet you is! *(She gives him a pinch.)*

DAVID: Don't know nuttin' 'bout dat.

GERSHOM: Feller grew up in Jenny Run-over's house an' he don't know nuttin' 'bout dat!

Everyone laughs. DAVID keeps working harder.

URIAH: Stop yur chatterin' all o' ye, an' look to yur work!

It's gittin' on to midnight, an' de Ole Testament says us cain't work on de Lord's day!

CASPER: If I had a wife an' kids, I wouldn't have dat Ole Testament roun' de house. All kinds o' filth in dere.

URIAH: Ahh Casper, ye don't talk nuttin' but flub-dub.

CASPER: It's full o' tales o' concubines an' kep' women an' ole whorin' stories!

URIAH: Don't be talkin' 'bout de Ole Testament like dat!

CASPER: But it's true! Ain't it, Uncle Sim?

CASPER kicks SIMEON.

SIMEON: Ay, dat's a fac', dat's a fac', dat's a fac'.

CASPER: Why, if e'er a child o' mine brung home a book wid stories like dat in it, I'd burn de book an' whip his arse.

URIAH: Stop jawin' or I'se'll whip yur arse, don't t'ink I couldn't!

JOSEPH: Sing us a piece, Gershom, would ye?

RUTH: Ay, Gershom, do. We needs somet'in' fur stren'th.

TAMAR: Sing us one ye made yur own self.

GERSHOM: I'se got a new one 'bout Casper ober dere.

FANNY: Ay, sing it Gershom! It's a good one. He sung it me las' night.

URIAH: Stop right dere, Gershom! I won't be hearin' no songs 'bout me nor none o' my kin. Not eben Casper. Us'll take a li'l res' if ye'll give us a drinkin' song, Gershom.

The group puts down their fish gear, saying: 'Ay,

a drinkin' song!' 'Ye got plenty o' dem, ain't ye?' 'Crank 'er out, Gershom!' etc.

GERSHOM: Alright, hush now, youse, I'se'll give ye a song. But ye bes' listen close.

All eyes turn to GERSHOM, who gathers himself for the performance.

GERSHOM: **When I grow old, and deat' comes callin'**
Don't lay my body in no hearse

Don't let de gals start caterwaulin'
Fur dat'll only make t'ings worse

Don't let no preacher preach no sermon
Fur I know my soul is cursed

Jus' dig a hole close to de ocean
Den whoeber gits dere first

Slip a jug o' rum inside my coffin
Case I wakes up wid a hellish t'irst

DAVID: I'se heard de fishermen singin' dat song! Ye made up dem words yur own self, Gershom?

GERSHOM: Dat I did.

JOSEPH: It's a gif' he has.

TAMAR: Ay. Gits it from his fader.

URIAH: Now, Gershom, if ye could only gib fish as good as ye kin make songs an' tell stories, ye'd be a great fisherman.

GERSHOM: I keeps my end up. I don't try to pull an' haul my

heart out like dis new feller, but I keeps my end up. 'Sides, I'se only bidin' my time workin' here 'til I inherits de lighthouse. In de meantime, I enjoys life, I does. Ain't dat right, Fanny?

FANNY: Ay, Gershom, ye does. Jus' ask any gal widin ten mile o' Rockbound!

GERSHOM: Twenny mile more like!

FANNY: Tell 'em what Molly Biddle says to ye las' week.

DAVID: Ay, Gershom, tell us.

GERSHOM: Las' Tuesday I t'ink it was, de night o' de big rainstorm. I'se feelin' right lonesome. So I sails ober de Outposts fur to visit my gals at Jenny Run-over's. Wid coins in my pocket, o' course. So I'se sittin' dere chattin' wid Jenny, havin' a couple drinks o' rum an' a pipe, when who comes out de back room but skinny Molly Biddle, nair a stitch o' clothes on 'er!

JOSEPH, CASPER & DAVID: No!

GERSHOM: Ay! An she says to me, 'Gershom, I'se got dis queer itch right here. Does ye t'ink ye could—

URIAH: Dat's enough, Gershom! My two darters is here, ain't it?

TAMAR: So what did ye do, Gershom?

FANNY: He gave 'er de Swedish scratch, didn't he?

FANNY and GERSHOM laugh.

RUTH: What's de Swedish scratch?

URIAH: Casper! More herrin' fur de gals!

GERSHOM: P'raps I'se'll show ye one day, Ruthie.

URIAH: Gershom! 'Nough dat blagardin'! We's gettin' close to de Sabbath. No more talkin'! Back to work!

Vocal rhythm comes back. Everyone gibs, but it's late, and the fish seem endless. They tire quickly, and their rhythm slows. Softly, through her fatigue, FANNY begins to sing.

FANNY: **Dere's a lan' dat is fairer dan day**
An' by fait' we can see it afar;
Fur de Fader waits ober de way
To prepare us a dwelling place dere.

ALL: **In de sweet by an' by**
We shall meet on dat beautiful shore
In de sweet by an' by
We shall meet on dat beautiful shore

The gibbing stops. Silence.

URIAH Dat's enough. Mus' be gettin' on fur midnight. Me nor me fader 'fore me nor his fader 'fore dat ne'er worked on de Lord's Day, an' I won't begin now. All hands to bed, says I. *(Everyone begins to exit.)* Hold on, David. You stay here, boy. Put de res' in pickle.

DAVID: But it's de Sabbath, an' ye said—

URIAH: No complainin' now. It'll only take a couple minutes—

DAVID: A couple hours, more like!

URIAH: An' tomorrow ye ain't doin' nuttin'. So git started!

As the others file out, an exhausted DAVID slowly starts scooping the unsplit herring into pickle tubs. After a moment, TAMAR sneaks back in and watches him work.

TAMAR: David?

DAVID sees her, says nothing, keeps working.

Ye needs any help, David? How 'bout you scoop up de herrin', an' I'se'll tip de pickle tubs. *(Pause.)* David?

DAVID: Don't need no help.

TAMAR: Suit yurself.

TAMAR pokes around, DAVID works.

Neber seen herrin' so t'ick 'roun' here. *(Pause.)* Casper reckons mus' be de tides.

DAVID: Dat's foolishness. Ain't got nuttin' to do wid no tides.

TAMAR: No, youse prob'ly right. Dat brudder o' mine's a big blow.

TAMAR walks over close to DAVID.

But I'se'll tell ye—us ain't neber seen herrin' so t'ick 'roun' here. *(Pause.)* P'r'aps it's all dat rain we had Tuesday las'. Ay, mus' be all dat rain.

DAVID: It ain't no rain, an' it ain't no tides. Sometimes herrin' jus' runs t'ick, dat's all.

TAMAR: True 'nuff, true 'nuff.

DAVID continues scooping herring.

Does ye t'ink could be on account o' all de extry sea dung?

DAVID: Dey ain't no extry sea dung, ye foolish gal!

TAMAR: I'se jus' tryin' to figure why herrin's runnin' so t'ick, David!

DAVID: Well, maybe ye has to ask de li'l buggers demselfs

why dey's runnin' so t'ick, 'cause I sure as hell don't know! *(Pause.)* Now, is dere anyt'in' else on yur mind?

TAMAR: As a matter of fac', I does have one oder question. *(Pause.)* David... ye eber been to Sweden?

DAVID stops working, looks at TAMAR. She smiles. DAVID drops his bucket.

Scene 4

Duren Bay. Three months later. Late evening. DAVID and GERSHOM are sailing back to Rockbound from Big Outpost in The Phoebe. *The water's calm and they're in no hurry. GERSHOM has a bottle of rum and a makeshift bandage around his head. GERSHOM staggers as he stands up with his bottle.*

GERSHOM: Dat Pierre Comeau t'inks he can play de fiddle? Sounds like a wrangy ole tomcat when he scrapes 'er! A wrangy ole tomcat lookin' fur a she-cat! Reeee-raaaaah, reeee-roooooh!

DAVID: But ye shouldn't o' t'rowed dat beer in Pierre's face, Gershom.

GERSHOM: Why not? Had it comin', tellin' me my fiddle playin' weren't no good. He's de one chowderin' de tunes!

DAVID: But ye wasted a whole glass o' black beer on de bugger! *(They laugh.)*

GERSHOM: Ye hear dem tunes I'se playin'? Got dem from a feller I met at Jenny's one night. Dem tunes is all de way from Denmark!

DAVID: Mus' be why dey sounded so queer.

GERSHOM: Kep' Boutilier's kitchen dancin', ain't I?

DAVID: Up'til Pierre smacked ye in de head.

GERSHOM: Well I paid him back, fis' right in de snotlocker!

DAVID: Ay, dat ye did! Knocked him on his arse!

GERSHOM: Boutilier shouldn't o' stopped us fightin', Davy. We was jus' gittin' started!

DAVID: But you two's de only fiddle players in de house. Break yur knuckles, ain't no more dancin'. An' only t'ing Boutilier likes better'n fightin' is dancin'.

GERSHOM: An' drinkin'.

DAVID: An' drinkin'.

GERSHOM takes a swig of rum, hands the bottle to DAVID.

GERSHOM: War'nt dat you out back grassin' wid Leah Levy?

DAVID: Ay. Dat lass sure is a looker, Gershom, ain't she?

GERSHOM: Cain't argey wid ye dere. But what ye goin' to do 'bout Uriah's gal?

DAVID: What ye mean, Uriah's gal?

GERSHOM: Talkin' 'bout Tamar. Seen 'er goin' in de fishhouse wid ye las' couple o' weeks, ain't I?

DAVID: Ah, dat ain't nuttin' but a bit o' fun. Tamar's a nice girl an' all, but I'se… Well, Gershom, I'se t'inkin' 'bout maybe one day marryin' dat Leah Levy.

GERSHOM: Marryin'?

DAVID: Her fader has eight t'ousand in de bank, dey say.

GERSHOM: Be a foggy Friday 'fore ye ketch me marryin'!

DAVID: An' he's got two hundred acres ober Little Outpost. Good land. I seen it!

GERSHOM: Well yur goin' to have to fish or cut bait, Davy. Two lasses at de same time ain't nuttin' but trouble.

DAVID: Reckon you'd know.

GERSHOM: Reckon I would.

The lighthouse light sweeps over them. GERSHOM looks toward it.

Dat's right, Fader
Keep 'er turnin', keep 'er turnin'
Ebery minute an' a half
Ebery minute an' a half
Fur de las' t'irty-eight year
Set yur clock by it, ye kin

Come close, Davy
Take a listen, take a listen
While we's floatin' in de bay
Talkin' foolish all de way
De light's whisperin' in our ear
Kin ye hear de words it says

The voice of the BARREN ISLAND LIGHTHOUSE is heard.

BARREN ISLAND LIGHTHOUSE: **I'se de Barren Island light**
I warn ye from de Rock
From de Grampus, from de Bull

Keep to de east'ard o' me
If ye hopes to make Minden by de inside passage

Keep to de west'ard if ye wants de ship's channel
'Twixt de Outposts to Duren Bay

I'se de Barren Island light
I warn ye from de Rock
From de Grampus, from de Bull

GERSHOM: **Eber seen de Bull, Davy?**
Snorts wid bot' nostrils, he does
Sprays high as de sky
An' roars somet'in' hellish
When he breaks

Steer ober de Bull, Davy
Dey ain't no use prayin'
Eben God up above
Won't dare journey down to de Bull

The lighthouse light sweeps over them.

Dat's right, Fader
Keep 'er turnin', keep 'er turnin'!
Ebery minute an' a half
Ebery minute an' a half
Fur de las' t'irty-eight year

GERSHOM sits, takes a drink of rum and lights a pipe.

DAVID: Ye t'ink de Grampus was once a green island like Rockbound, Gershom? Ye t'ink one day dese islands goin' to be black shoals? God's in de land, devil's in de ocean, I reckon, an' dey's havin' a hellish struggle. God's tryin' to build 'er up, give us some land to put our feet on, a place to make a life.

Devil growls an' roars, tryin' to destroy what we got, tryin' to take away de islands an' de mainlan'.

Whene'er Jenny Run-over had a few drinks in her, Lord, she'd say how youse de great lover o' men. If dat's true, why'd ye make life so rough an' hard? Why don't you stop dat devil when he's pullin' men to de bottom o' de sea, makin' all dem widders and orphans? Why's dogfish and albacore got to ruin our nets? Why's sharks got to give us fear in de night? Ole Uncle Uriah, he claims to be God-fearin'. Neber works on de Sabbath. Lets me do it fur 'im! Why's he so graspin', makin' me work day an' night, stealin' my money wheneber he gets de chance? He's got more money'n he'll eber need. An' why's I hardly got none? All I want's to paint my house, git some nice clothes, maybe marry dat Leah Levy an' buy me a fiddle so's I kin play a few jigs like Pierre Comeau. Lord, Pierre plays somet'in' fierce on dat fiddle!

DAVID sees that GERSHOM has fallen asleep.

P'r'aps one day, if I gits some good money, I'se'll buy my own boat an' I won't have to answer to nobody. Not eben Uncle Uriah.

But til' dat day

I still wants to t'ank ye, Lord

Fur black beer

An' fur dancin'

An' fur fightin'

An' fur de fish in de sea

An' fur de sof' crowberry

Dat Leah Levy an' I like to lie on

When us's grassin'

An' fur de Sabbath

So we gits at leas' one day o' res'

Don't let 'em eber change dat, Lord

An' las' of all

I t'anks ye fur de sun in de day to warm us

An' de stars at night to guide us

DAVID's gaze shifts toward the lighthouse.

DAVID: Seems to me I ain't seen de light circlin'?

Long pause. DAVID nudges GERSHOM, who's still sleeping.

Gershom! It should o' come 'roun' by now. *(Pause.)* Gershom, it's gone out, I tell ye!

GERSHOM wakes.

GERSHOM: What? What ye talkin'?

DAVID: De light! De light's out on Barren Island!

GERSHOM looks toward the light.

GERSHOM: Start de engine up, Davy. Nail 'er to de pin!

DAVID revs the motor. They head toward Barren Island.

Scene 5

That night. TAMAR and FANNY are in the fishhouse. FANNY's peeling potatoes.

TAMAR: Bugger said he'd be here, Fanny. Tole me his own self he'd be here tonight! Arter Boutilier's dance. Knew I should o' gone wid!

FANNY: Him an' Gershom's prob'ly jus' kickin' up some trouble ober Boutilier's. Davy'll be here soon enough, gal. T'ree sheets to de wind, p'r'aps, but he'll be here. Why don't ye peel a couple o' taters? Helps pass de hours. Us's makin' kuduffle soup in de mornin', so we—

TAMAR: I tole him I'se got to talk wid! What's de time, Fanny? Midnight? Mus' be arter midnight, I lays!

FANNY: Neber seen ye so growly, girl. What is it? *(TAMAR turns away.)* Dis young feller's gittin' under yer skin, ain't he? What ye see in dat boy?

TAMAR: He's a smart lad.

FANNY: Davy? He ain't neber larned readin' nur numbers, Tamar. What ye talkin'?

TAMAR: **In de middle o' de night**
When him an' I'se reclinin'
An' de moon is burnin' bright
So we starts intertwinin'
He keeps de curtains drawn up tight
So dat moon dat's brightly shinin'
Doesn't give us bot' away
'Cause if we had our drudders
Don't want no coitus interruptus
From me fader or me brudders
Ay, he's a smart lad

An' on dis stubborn ole island
Dis hellhole name o' Rockbound
Ain't no-one can touch him
When it comes to fishin'
Some says dey kin
But dey's only wishin'

Eben Casper an' Joseph
Me hypocrite brudders
Dey keep dere eyes wide open
Sailin' out o' Rockboun'
Jus' a-hopin' to see
Where Davy's hunkerin' down
Den when he tosses his anchor
Dat's when dey bot' circle roun'
Fur dey know dey'll be
Plenny o' cod to be foun' dere
Ay, he's a smart lad

A sound from offstage of someone approaching.

FANNY: Dere he is, gal. Tole ye he'd be back. *(Yelling off.)* David, Gershom wid ye?

URIAH: *(Offstage.)* It ain't David, an' it ain't Gershom!

FANNY: Yur fader! Bes' hide, gal. Quick!

TAMAR hides behind a puncheon. URIAH enters.

URIAH: Waitin' fur a man all hours de night. In de fishhouse, eben! Ain't proper fur a gal, Fanny. Ain't proper.

FANNY: I'se jus' peelin' taters fur kuduffle soup, Uriah, dat's all. What you doin' down here?

URIAH: Cain't sleep fur t'inkin' bout dat damn David Jung. Bugger ought to be home sleepin'. He knows us's workin' in de mornin'! Mos' times I neber lets dese sharesmen rile me up. But dis one—he's got me barkin' a blue breeze!

Cain't seem to wear dat hellion down
Not Casper wid his taunts
Nor Joseph stealin' half

His lobster pots whene'er he wants
I eben tried las' week
To skeer him off wid fearsome haunts
An' now he's bought a piece o' waterfront
Just ober to de west
He eben bought it from a Kraus
Dat harpy Anapest!
Oh, he's a smart lad

An' in my beautiful kingdom
Dis island name o' Rockbound
Ain't no-one can touch him
When it comes to fishin'
Dey ain't got de guts
Dey ain't got no ambition
Look at Casper an' Joseph
Me lazy-arse offspring
Dey keep dere eyes wide open
Sailin' out o' Rockboun'
Jus' a-hopin' to see
Where Davy's hunkerin' down
Den when he tosses his anchor
Dat's when dey bot' circle roun'
Fur dey know dey'll be
Plenny o' cod to be foun' dere
Oh, he's a smart lad

URIAH kicks the puncheon. TAMAR is hiding behind. TAMAR yelps, surprising URIAH.

Krily kripse, Tamar, ye near skeered de bejesus out o' me. What you doin' back dere?

TAMAR: I'se jus' helpin' Fanny wid taters, fur kuduffle soup Fader, an…an den you—

URIAH: Don't give me no kuduffle soup! Youse waitin' here fur dat scoundrel David Jung, ain't ye?

TAMAR: Well?

URIAH: Dat settles it. Come wid! I'se gittin' rid o' David tomorrow, come hell or high water. Don't care how many fish he ketches!

TAMAR: No! Ye cain't do dat!

URIAH: On dis here island I does what I damn well pleases!

TAMAR: Maybe so, but you cain't get rid o' David.

URIAH: Why de hell not?

TAMAR: Trus' me, Fader, youse goin' to have to get used to de lad.

URIAH: *(Pause.)* What you sayin', gal?

FANNY: Tamar? Youse—

TAMAR: I is.

Scene 6

That night. Barren Island lighthouse. A ladder leads to an upper level where the light is situated. The light is out. DAVID and GERSHOM are barely discernible, slowly entering the room, closing the door. GERSHOM is carrying his bottle of rum. DAVID uses a match to light a lantern. We see an overturned table and OLD GERSHOM lying dead on the floor, a half-emptied jug of rum in his hand. GERSHOM cries out and runs to him, holds him.

GERSHOM: Fader! Look at his face, Davy, look at his face!

Reckon he was strugglin'. Strugglin' somet'in' fierce wid a…a hellish haunt when he died! O Lord… Fader…

GERSHOM holds him close, trembling with grief and terror.

DAVID: Don't know 'bout no haunts, Gershom, but dey's sailors out dere, close to de shore! Youse got to light de lamp. Gershom! No time to was'e! *(Pause. GERSHOM doesn't move.)* Gershom, haunts or no, youse de lighthouse keeper now.

GERSHOM looks at DAVID, slowly rises. GERSHOM takes a drink of rum. Then he and DAVID ascend the ladder and relight the lamp.

GERSHOM: **Youse right, Davy**

Keep 'er turnin', keep 'er turnin', I will!

Ebery minute an' a half

Ebery minute an' a half

Fur de nex' t'irty-eight year

Set dere clocks by it, dey will

Scene 7

URIAH's fish house. The next day.

URIAH: **Scrawny whelp like you sneaks out here an' chases arter my darter!**

DAVID: Us's only foolin' 'roun', Uriah. Ain't nuttin'—

URIAH: **Knocked up, she is.**

DAVID: What?

URIAH: **An' here's one o' Nicolas Kaulbach's boys**

Bin a-wantin' her dis two year

Him what owns a fish stand an' forty acres o' good ground!

DAVID: Nick's boy kin still have her, Uriah.

URIAH: **Youse talkin' flub-dub**
Nicolas Kaulbach's boy won't want her now
Will he?
De only one to marry Tamar is you
Ain't it?

DAVID: **Ain't dis a pretty kettle o' fish?**
Ye needs me to marry yur darter
Ain't dis a pretty kettle o' fish?
Well, let's set de date:
How's about when cod learn to fly?

URIAH: **Dey's no bastards in dis here family**

DAVID: **I'se'll pay de bill fur de doctor**

URIAH: **Youse de only one Tamar kin marry**

DAVID **I'se not earnin' near 'nuff money**

URIAH **Ye'd make more money if ye worked a li'l harder**

Pause. DAVID thinks.

DAVID: Take me into de firm.

URIAH: What?

DAVID: I bin sharesman now near half a year an' I'se ketched more fish dan air Joe or Casper. Take me into de firm on an even divvy, an' I'se'll marry Tamar.

URIAH: Ye come here a beggar an now ye wants in my firm what me an' my fader made?

DAVID: I need somet'in' to pass down to my kid same as

you an' yur fader afore ye. I'se a Jung an' de same blood as you.

URIAH: Holy ole twis', ye certainly got de gall!

DAVID: Does ye want me to marry Tamar, or does ye want to raise a Jung bastard?

URIAH: I wants you off dis island. Ye ain't no sharesman wid me no more!

DAVID: Sharesman or no, I won't get off dis island. I'se'll build me own launch an' fish house on de land what Anapest sold me an' I'se'll hire me own damn sharesmen.

URIAH: Casper tole me youse a scoundrel. Should o' listened!

DAVID: I don't wish Tamar no harm, Uriah. She's a good gal, but she ain't de woman fur me.

URIAH fumes, paces.

Ye t'ink it ober. If ye wants Tamar married, ye takes me into de firm on an even divvy.

URIAH continues pacing.

T'ink it ober, Uriah, an'—

URIAH: I'se'll take ye into de firm on de line fish an' herrin', but ye'll go sharesman on de mackerel.

DAVID: Why on de mackerel?

URIAH: 'Cause ye ain't got no mackerel gear.

DAVID: I'se'll t'ink 'bout it.

URIAH: Ye says right now. Dere ain't no time fur delays. If you'se goin' to marry Tamar it's got to be right off. Den we kin spread de word 'twere a seben mont's' child.

DAVID : How 'bout lobsters?

URIAH: Sharesman on lobsters too.

DAVID: No. Lobsterin's too heavy an' dangerous. I won't go dat lay. I wants my own lobsters.

URIAH: Den keep yur own lobsters what ye ketches in yur own traps what ye make wid yur own damn hands. What kind o' man is ye, anyhow? First ye knocks up me gal, an' den, instead o' bein' sorry an' repentant, ye drives a hard bargain ober it!

DAVID: I'se a man what stands up fur me rights an' tears away what I kin git from people like ye. Didn't ye try fur to keep me off dis island an' part of it mine by right?

URIAH: Rockbound was mine alone 'til ye an' Anapest come sneakin' back on it! Me an' my fader made dis island what it is, ain't it?

DAVID: An' me grandfader, he made it, too!

URIAH: Well, it's no good argeyin' wid a t'ickhead like you. Is it a bargain? Does ye marry Tamar?

DAVID: If I gits a divvy on all but de mackerel.

DAVID and URIAH shake hands.

Scene 8

Barren Island Lighthouse. Early evening. Three months later. GERSHOM is pacing, jittery.

GERSHOM: **One crow is sorrow**

Two crows joy

T'ree crows a weddin'

Four crows a boy

Five crows silver

Six crows gold

Seben crows a story neber to be told

A sound from offstage. GERSHOM starts, looks out the window, calls out.

Krily kripse, Davy, where ye been? Come a horn onto de line, tie 'er up an' haul yur carcass in here!

GERSHOM grabs a jug of rum from the table.

One crow is sorrow

Two crows joy

T'ree crows a weddin'

Four crows a boy

Five crows silver

Six crows gold

Seben crows a story neber to be told

DAVID enters, takes off his rain gear. GERSHOM runs over, embraces him.

By de rattly-eyed Jesus, youse a pretty sight, Davy, a real pretty sight! T'ought ye'd be here dis afternoon!

DAVID: Hell of a trip, Gershom. Growlers eberywhere dis time o' year. An' it's a big rough out dere.

GERSHOM: What you doin' paddlin' yur li'l yaller dory?

DAVID: Ole Uriah wouldn't let me take *De Phoebe*. Says, 'You want to go a-drinkin', ye ain't takin' my boat.'

GERSHOM: Ole bastard. Sit down, sit down, have a draught.

GERSHOM hands him the rum. DAVID drinks.

Funny t'ing, but I'se been goin' a li'l half-crazed, Davy, dese las' couple o' mont's. Don't know how

Fader did it all dem years. Naught to do but t'ink out here.

DAVID: Youse mudder soul alone in dis lighthouse, ain't ye?

GERSHOM: Jus' me an' dem haunts dat spooks me ebery night. Dey's hard to git used to, Davy.

DAVID: Beginnin's always toughest, ain't it? Have ye t'ought 'bout growin' somethin'? Bit o' timothy, or a mowin' field, or eben a couple o' bushes? Island's awful somber-lookin'.

GERSHOM: Fader tried. Won't nuttin' grow. All dat salt spray an' droppin's from de careys.

DAVID: Well, it's bound to git easier wid passage o' time.

GERSHOM: Reckon so. *(GERSHOM takes a drink.)*

DAVID: *(Pause.)* Ole Uriah ain't too happy 'bout losin' you as sharesman. He's always krexin' how Joseph should o' got dis lighthouse.

GERSHOM: He wants de eighty dollars a mont' for hisself!

DAVID: Youse right dere!

GERSHOM: Bah, I don't care naught 'bout none o' dem Jungs! 'Cept you, Davy. You's de only good one 'mongst 'em. Fanny miss me?

DAVID: Fanny? Talks 'bout nuttin' but Gershom dis, Gershom dat. Why don't ye marry de gal, bring her out? Might cheer de place.

GERSHOM: No, dat ain't fur me. Marryin's fur fellas like you. Fellas ain't got no sense.

DAVID: Marryin' Tamar's turned out pretty darn good. Ain't naught better'n hapjacks in de mornin', a lunch o' bread an' cakes all wrapped in a white cloth, packed in a tin box to take to de banks. Clean sheets on de bed, clean underclothes by de kitchen fire of a Sunday mornin'. An' I likes bein part o' de firm, Gershom, workin' fur me own divvy. Sure, Joseph an' Casper still tries to steal what dey kin, but Tamar, she's smart. She knows readin', an' numbers. She keeps an eye open so dem Jung boys has to give me what I got comin'. When I goes home tomorrow, ye know what's waitin' fur me? A good dinner to warm me belly an' a good woman to warm me bed. An' in a couple o' months I'se going to be a fader!

GERSHOM: A fader? Reckon ye're ready fur yur own li'l wharf rat?

DAVID: Weren't too keen at firs', but I'se likin' de idea now.

GERSHOM: Well here's to ye, Davy, ye ole christer. Hope yur spawn comes out wid more sense n' you got! Divel a bissel, I'se dry as a las' year's robin's nest.

GERSHOM takes a drink. Wind is heard howling.

DAVID: Lord liftin', it's blowin' like hell dis ebenin'!

GERSHOM: Ay. It's a rare night fur ghos's.

DAVID: I lays de footless sailor's flittin' dis night on Rockbound.

GERSHOM: Dere's somethin' queer on dis island, too, Davy. Come from de Sanford folks.

DAVID: De Sanford folks?

GERSHOM: You mind Johnny Publicover, de ghos' catcher on Big Outpost?

DAVID: I minds him well, 'cause I lived nigh him when I was a gaffer. Youse talkin' 'bout de... *(DAVID smiles.)* de Sanford ghos', ain't ye, Gershom?

GERSHOM offers DAVID the rum, lemon, sugar and hot water and takes some himself, all very deliberately. DAVID makes his hot toddy, takes a sip and settles in for the tale. The ENSEMBLE steps forward to help in the storytelling, occasionally enacting parts of it.

GERSHOM: **Well, I reckon ye recall how de Sanford ghos'**

Had de women an' de children an' de men folk too

All skeert,

Dat skeert, dey was hackin' up dere hapjacks

Messin' up dere metzelsuppe

Eben talkin' 'bout gittin' out o' Sanford

Maybe eben movin' to de islands

An' dey's mainland folk!

Dis ghos' was rollin' big beach rocks up an' down de hallways

Snatchin' pretty lasses when dey's grassin' in de ebenin'

Whangin' on de church while de preacher's talkin'

(Talkin' 'bout flub-dub)

So one Sunday mornin' dis here preacher was a-preachin' 'bout de

Evils o' de bottle when de Sanford ghos'

He gits dat bold

He reaches t'rough de winder wid a skinny li'l arm

An' den down on de pulpit

What's dat?

A nice glass o' rum fur de preacher man!

GERSHOM pours a hot toddy and drinks.

Dat wery audacious Sanford ghos'!

ENSEMBLE: Dat wery audacious Sanford ghos'!

DAVID: Dat wery audacious Sanford ghos'!

ENSEMBLE: Dat wery audacious Sanford ghos'!

GERSHOM: So Hermione Slaughenwhite stands up tall
In de church an' she says:

HERMIONE: I'se had enough o' dis wery audacious Sanford ghos'
Rollin' big beach rocks up an' down de hallways
Snatchin' pretty lasses when dey's grassin' in de ebenin'
Whangin' on de church while de preacher's talkin'
(Talkin' 'bout flub-dub)

It's time to git a ghos' ketcher
Dat's right!
You know de wery feller I'se a-talkin' about
Johnny Publicover!

ENSEMBLE: Johnny Publicover! Johnny Publicover!

PREACHER: No!
Dat man ain't nuttin' but a stinkin' ole lyin' ole witch!
If he goes oogy-boogy on ye
Why he kin crack yur yoke an' yur harness all to pieces
Or cover yur boat wid a mess o' salty barnacles

ENSEMBLE: Johnny Publicover! Johnny Publicover!
Johnny Publicover! Johnny Publicover!
Johnny Publicover!

PREACHER: **Wid de power o' prayer**
An' de stren'th o' de Lord
We kin exorcise dis ghos' ourselves!

HERMIONE: **Dis here ghos' gits plenny enough exercise**
Grassin' wid de lasses!

GERSHOM: **Den whang! whang! whang! on de back o' dat church**

ENSEMBLE: **Whang! whang! whang! on de back o' dat church**

GERSHOM: **Critter damn nigh bust right in t'rough de wall**

ENSEMBLE: **Critter damn nigh bust right in t'rough de wall**

GERSHOM: **So de Sanford folks reckon dey's had enough o' dis**
Rollin' big beach rocks up an' down de hallways
Snatchin' pretty lasses when dey's grassin' in de ebenin'
Whangin' on de church while de preacher's talkin'

ALL: **(Talkin' 'bout flub-dub)**

GERSHOM: **Nuttin' fur to do but to call in de ghos' ketcher**

JOHNNY PUBLICOVER enters with a big net, a duck gun and a large canvas bag with a drawstring. GERSHOM and DAVID take long drinks.

ENSEMBLE: **John, Johnny, Johnny Pub, Johnny Public, Johnny Publicover!**
John, Johnny, Johnny Pub, Johnny Public, Johnny Publicover!
John, Johnny, Johnny Pub, Johnny Public, Johnny Publicover!
John, Johnny, Johnny Pub, Johnny Public, Johnny Publicover!

JOHNNY
PUBLICOVER: **Here I is, Hermione!**

ENSEMBLE: **Johnny Publicover!**

JOHNNY
PUBLICOVER: **Here I is, preacher!**

ENSEMBLE: **John, Johnny, Johnny Pub, Johnny Public, Johnny Publicover!**

JOHNNY
PUBLICOVER: **So where's dis wery audacious Sanford ghos'?**

Bring him out, bring him out right now

I'll shoot him in de arse

Whack him in de head

Slip him in me net

An' stick him in me bag

Same's I did all de oder ones, oder ones

Same's I did all de oder ones

All I needs is

Five dollar

The ENSEMBLE pool their resources and give JOHNNY PUBLICOVER his five dollars.

ENSEMBLE: **Johnny Publicover! Johnny Publicover!**

Johnny Publicover! Johnny Publicover!

Johnny Publicover!

GERSHOM: **Den whang! whang! whang! on de back o' dat church once more**

ENSEMBLE: **Whang! whang! whang! on de back o' dat church once more**

JOHNNY PUBLICOVER exits with his weapons to get the SANFORD GHOST.

GERSHOM: **Dat wery audacious Sanford ghos'!**

ENSEMBLE: **Dat wery audacious Sanford ghos'!**

DAVID: **Dat wery audacious Sanford ghos'!**

ENSEMBLE: **Dat wery audacious Sanford ghos'!**

ALL: **Dat wery audacious Sanford ghos'!**
Dat wery audacious Sanford ghos'!
Dat—

A big bang from offstage. JOHNNY PUBLICOVER enters with something in his large canvas bag that is kicking and squirming.

JOHNNY PUBLICOVER: **Here's yur ghos', an' he weren't dat tough**

HERMIONE: **Jus' look at him a-kickin' an'**
A-scratchin' an' a-strangulatin'!

SANFORD GHOST: **Raah! Ree!**
Raah! Ree!

JOHNNY PUBLICOVER: **I kotch 'em far, far worser nor dis one**

SANFORD GHOST: **Raah! Ree!**
Raah! Ree!

ENSEMBLE: **How did ye git him, Johnny?**
How did ye git him?

JOHNNY PUBLICOVER: **Shot him in de arse**
Jus' like I said
Den I chased him t'rough de bushes

An' I whacked him on de head

Slipped him in me net

Stuck him in me bag

Same's I did all de oder ones, oder ones

Same's I did all de oder ones

SANFORD GHOST: **Raah! Ree!**

JOHNNY PUBLICOVER kicks the SANFORD GHOST to shut him up.

JOHNNY PUBLICOVER: **An' dat's dat!**

DAVID: An' what you s'pose he had in dat bag, now, Gershom?

GERSHOM: I don't need to s'pose, I knows, 'cause I was tole by me fader hisself. An' de ole man—he weren't no fool.

It were dat wery audacious Sanford ghos'!

HERMIONE: **I'se goin' to finish off de bugger right now**

Gimme dat gun, gimme dat gun!

HERMIONE grabs JOHNNY PUBLICOVER's gun and aims it at the sack. The SANFORD GHOST squirms more violently.

SANFORD GHOST: **What?**

JOHNNY PUBLICOVER: **No, Hermione**

Put dat down!

Ye cain't finish off no ghos' like dis wid a gun!

Ye gots to take him to a far off island

Out in de middle o' de deep blue sea

An' leave de bugger stranded dere fureber an' fureber!

ENSEMBLE: **An' leave de bugger stranded dere fureber an' fureber!**

GERSHOM: **So Johnny Publicover told Hermione an' de preacher**

An' de rest o' dem Sanford folks

Dat he'd de ghos' to a far off island

Out in de middle o' de deep blue sea

An' leave de bugger stranded dere fureber an' fureber!

ENSEMBLE: **Johnny Publicover! Johnny Publicover!**

Johnny Publicover!

GERSHOM: **All he'd be needin' was:**

JOHNNY PUBLICOVER: **Anoder five dollar**

GERSHOM: So Johnny got his money an' de wery nex' day, de Sanford folks rowed off wid Johnny an' de ghos' still a-flutterin' an a-squawkin' in dat bag. An' where d'ye s'pose dey landed dat haunt?

DAVID: Don't know, Gershom. Where?

GERSHOM: *(Pause'silence.)* Right here on Barren Island, Davy. Dat's where dey lef' dat wery audacious Sanford ghos'. Dat were 'fore de light were built, an dere war'nt no human habitations.

DAVID: So dat ghos' is roamin' dis island still?

GERSHOM: Many a night ye kin see him stretched out flat on de coffin stones, a-moanin' like all possessed an' grievin' fur his ancient home in Sanford.

They listen. Wind blows.

DAVID: Time to turn in, I reckon.

GERSHOM: Turn in? Why? You'se dead when you'se asleep. Have anoder drink, Davy. I ain't seen a livin' soul close to t'ree mont's.

DAVID: Well, s'pose one more draught couldn't hurt none.

GERSHOM: Dat's it, one li'l nightcap, den we turn in. *(GERSHOM pours them a drink. Wind gusts dangerously, shaking the windows.)* Kripse! What's dat? *(He hurries to the window, takes a look out.)* What de hell? Ain't nuttin'? *(GERSHOM laughs.)* 'Fraid we ain't gittin' no sleep, lad. Sanford ghos' goin' to have a li'l fun wid us tonight.

DAVID: Sanford ghos'?

GERSHOM: Sometimes he rattles me winders de whole night long, he does.

DAVID: So what'll we do, Gershom?

GERSHOM: Reckon we's got no choice but to stay up an' finish off dat jug.

GERSHOM pours himself a drink, downs it in one gulp, pours another. He's now feeling the effects of the liquor.

Ye kin take a look at one o' me fader's books if ye like.

DAVID: Cain't read 'em.

GERSHOM: Dey's plenny o' pictures in 'em.

DAVID walks toward the bookshelf.

But watch where yur goin', Davy. Ober dere, behind dat bookshelf? Dey's a black an' yaller dog sometimes come out, snarlin' like de devil. I only sees him on de wane o' de moon.

GERSHOM staggers over to the window, looks at the moon.

An' it's wanin' tonight.

DAVID: A black an' yaller dog? But Gershom, dey ain't no—

GERSHOM: *(Softly, to himself.)*

One crow is sorrow

Two crows joy

T'ree crows a weddin'

Four crows a—

You sure youse got to go tomorrow mornin', Davy?

DAVID: Ay. Uriah's got me workin'. An' Anapest says Tamar shouldn't do too much on her own. She's bin feelin' kind o' sickly on account o' de kid comin'.

GERSHOM: Love dat gal, don't ye?

DAVID: Reckon I does.

GERSHOM: Dat's good fur ye, Davy. Real good.

DAVID: Youse goin' to come visitin', Gershom, ain't ye? Out to Rockbound?

GERSHOM: Too much work here. Cain't leave.

DAVID: P'r'aps ye kin come an' have Christmas dinner wid.

GERSHOM: Maybe, lad, if dey's no ice.

Scene 9

The next evening. Duren Bay. DAVID is rowing vigourously in his yellow dory. He's heading back from Barren Island toward Rockbound. The bay is rough. A beam of light makes a circular sweep through his path.

DAVID: **Dat's right, Gershom**

Keep 'er turnin', keep 'er turnin'

Fur tonight de breakers roll

So guide me safely past de shoal

So's I kin make my way home

An' I kin kiss my lass good night

Another beam of light cuts through his path. Lights come up on TAMAR lying in bed, talking to URIAH.

TAMAR: Fader, I don't feel so good. *(TAMAR groans in pain.)* T'ink you'd bes' git Anapest, Fader!

URIAH: *(Calling downstairs.)* Anapest! Anapest, git up here!

ANAPEST enters.

TAMAR: Anapest, t'ank de Lord.

ANAPEST: What is it child?

TAMAR: Don't know, but I t'ink I feels de pains comin' on me.

TAMAR moans again. Another beam of light sweeps the stage. Lights down on TAMAR. DAVID is rowing faster.

DAVID: **One tent' o' de island o' Rockbound is mine, now**

Mine by law, mine by law

Pass t'rough me, when I dies, now

To my son, my eldest son

Another beam of light cuts through his path. Lights up on TAMAR, ANAPEST and URIAH. TAMAR is in pain.

ANAPEST: Where's David, Tamar? We need him here.

TAMAR : He's ober Barren Island.

ANAPEST: What in hell's he doin' ober Barren Island?

URIAH: He's drinkin' an' carousin' wid dat Gershom, dat's what!

TAMAR: Said he'd be back dis mornin'. Don't know what happened.

ANAPEST: Big bottle o' rum's what happened, I lays.

TAMAR: Somet'in' don't feel right, Anapest. Somet'in jus' don't feel—

TAMAR groans.

ANAPEST: Alright, child, take dis. *(She puts a cloth on her forehead.)* Uriah, git me anoder bucket o' water, quick.

URIAH: If ye t'ink jus' 'cause youse fam'ly ye kin order me aroun' whene'er ye—

TAMAR screams.

ANAPEST: Git goin', Uriah! An' call Fanny!

URIAH exits. Another beam of light sweeps the stage. DAVID's rowing still faster.

TAMAR: **Where's Fader, Anapest?**

DAVID: **One tent' o' de island o' Rockbound is mine, now**

TAMAR: **Where's Fanny, Anapest?**

DAVID: **Mine by law, mine by law**

TAMAR: **Where's Casper, Anapest?**

DAVID: **Pass t'rough me, when I dies, now**

TAMAR: **Where's David, Anapest?**

DAVID: **To my son, my eldest son**

TAMAR: **Anapest?**

TAMAR dies. ANAPEST holds her newborn son. The ENSEMBLE gathers around TAMAR.

ENSEMBLE: **One crow is sorrow**
Two crows joy
T'ree crows a weddin'
Four crows a boy
Five crows silver
Six crows gold
Seben crows a story neber to be told

DAVID is still rowing.

End of Act I.

Act II

Scene 1

A year and a half later. In the new school house. Both Rockbound clans are present. Representing the JUNGS: URIAH, CASPER, JOSEPH and his new wife, ALMA. Representing the KRAUSES: ANAPEST, CHRISTIAN and MELCHER. There is an air of silent distrust as the two clans eye each other. DAVID is sitting at the back. CASPER has a book of procedural rules that he refers to occasionally. FANNY is attempting to chair the meeting.

FANNY: **Well, we's gaddered up all o' ye Jungs an' Krauses**

An' put ye all togedder in de bery same room

Eben got ole Uriah here an' Anapest too

Hardly neber see de two o' ye face to face

'Less we's habin' us a birt' or a deat' on de island

URIAH: **I neber did relish de sight o' dat homely ole catfish**

ANAPEST: **Watch what ye're sayin', Ury**

'Less dis ole catfish pulls de whiskers off o' yur face!

FANNY: **Alright! Dat dere's enuff!**

I instrucks ye bot' to ack cordial now

'Cause I'se de chairman o' dis here meetin'

JOSEPH: Why's dat potato-gal git to be de chairman, Fader? I'd do it better.

URIAH: Hush, now, Joseph. Chairman don't git no vote.

CASPER: *(Points to his book of procedure.)* 'Less dey's a tie.

URIAH: *(Mocking.)* ...'Less dey's a tie... Ye always knows all de li'l rules an' reg'lations, don't ye?

ANAPEST: Fanny makes de bes' chairman on account o' she's de only one on dis island dat she ain't no Kraus an' she ain't no Jung neider. Now git on wid it, lass.

FANNY: **Well, now, eberyone open up yur eyes, take a good look 'round**

We'se finally built our bery firs' school house

Took damn near to a year an' a half

Built real strong, an' it looks smart too

But it ain't no use 'til we gits us a teacher

An' to choose a teacher, we'se got to elect a...

What's it called agin', Casper?

CASPER: **A secretary-treasurer**

FANNY: **A secretary-treasurer**

So's he kin start to makin' de...

Casper?

CASPER: **De tax assessments**

FANNY: **De tax assessments**

URIAH: **Hold on!**

Don't like de sound o' dat!

CASPER: Fader, I'se already tole ye: We'se got to collec' taxes so's we kin pay dis teacher her salary.

CHRISTIAN: She ain't goin' to larn de childer fur free, Uriah.

MELCHER: Durn right she ain't.

URIAH: Me fader nor his fader 'fore dat didn't need no readin' nor writin'. Dis here school's goin' to bring us naught but trouble!

ANAPEST: Dear dyin' Moses, Ury. School's standin' up tall, all built, ain't it? Ye want to tear 'er back down agin'? Let's start votin' so's we kin go home.

I nominates fur secretary-treasurer my firs'-born—Christian Kraus.

FANNY: Christian Kraus it is. Any oders?

URIAH: **I nominates me own firs'-born—Casper Jung**

FANNY: Casper Jung is de second. Any more? No? Den I guess we's got to vote. Who's partial to Casper Jung?

URIAH, CASPER and JOSEPH raise there hands.

Dat's t'ree fur Casper. Who's partial to Christian Kraus?

CHRISTIAN and MELCHER raise their hands.

Well, s'pose dat means it's—

ANAPEST: Hold yur taters, Fanny.

ANAPEST raises her hand.

FANNY: Uh, yes, Anapest. Ye got somet'in to say?

ANAPEST: No, I'se votin'.

Pause. Everyone looks at ANAPEST.

URIAH: Women ain't got no vote in dis meetin', Anapest. Ye know dat full well. It ain't natural, it ain't allowed in no land nowhere.

ANAPEST: Natural fur women to have naught to say, is it?

URIAH: Dat's right.

ANAPEST: Ain't ye neber heard tell o' Victoria, Queen of England, Ury? Or ole Queen Elizabeth? Bot' o' dem gals had a t'ing or two to say, an' folks listened.

URIAH: We ain't electin' no queens here tonight.

ANAPEST: True 'nuff, we'se electin' a secretary-treasurer. An' don't I own land an' pay fur dis teacher same as de res' o' youse? Cain't I haul a line an' lug a barrow good as air a man on Rockbound? Tell me, does pants make ye vote? Many's de warm night when I strips off nekkid, wearin' nuttin' but oil pants in de fish house!

MELCHER: Mudder, please—

ANAPEST: Melcher, gimme yur trousers. Ury says it's pants make ye vote, reckon I'se'll have to put some on!

ANAPEST starts to pull off her clothes.

URIAH: Krily kripse, Anapest, go ahead an' vote if ye has to, but leave yur durn petticoats on!

ANAPEST: *(Buttoning back up.)* I votes fur me son, Christian.

CASPER: *(Pointing to JOSEPH's wife.)* If women gits a vote, Fader, den Alma gits a vote too.

URIAH: Dat's right. Alma—put up yur hand.

ALMA: Me?

URIAH: Ye're a part o' dis family too since ye married Joseph.

ALMA: But Uriah, I don't know nuttin' 'bout—

URIAH: I said put up yur hand, gal! *(ALMA puts up her hand.)* Dere, she's votin' fur Casper, it's four to t'ree, now let's get on with it.

DAVID: Hold on. *(Pause.)* I own land, I gits a vote at dis meetin' too, ain't it?

URIAH: Reckon ye los' all yur rights dat cold night las' year.

DAVID: **It's true, I ain't said much since dat night**
Let de res' o' youse make de decisions
Ain't felt I had no right

But we's talkin' here 'bout de school house
Who's goin' to teach de childer?
Who's goin' to keep our money safe?

An' my li'l one, Ralph
He'll be comin' here
In a couple year
So I got no choice
Got to speak up

Don't want my boy to end up trapped on dis rock
Wranglin' day an' night wid ye Jungs an' ye Krauses
Listenin' to ye bicker an' squawk

Ralphie's goin' to do as he wants to
Sure, I'se'll teach him fishin'
Ain't nuttin' I cain't larn him dere

But unlike his dad
He's goin' to also larn
How to read a book
So's he'll know de names
Of all de Kings of England

An' he'll write down words
An' he'll play de piano
An' he's damn well goin' to know numbers
Like Tamar done
I'se votin' fur Christian Kraus.

FANNY: Reckon dat means we's got a tie.

CASPER: An' like I says afore, Fader if ye had o' bin listenin'—'Cordin' to dese here rules, a tie gits broke by de chairman.

FANNY: De chairman' But, but—I don't want to cast no vote, I—

URIAH: Don't fergit who it was firs' hired ye on out here, Fanny. When ye're votin', don't fergit where yur bread gits buttered!

ANAPEST: Dey ain't no choice a tall, Fanny. Take a look at de two boys. Who'd ye trus' wid yur money? Dat Casper?

DAVID: Stan' back, youse, an' let de gal cogitate! What'll it be, Fanny?

FANNY: Kripse, Davy, I don't know— *(Pause.)* Christian.

URIAH: Baaah!

ANAPEST: Dat's my gal! Christian, come on up here. No p'int wastin' time, firs' t'ing ye do is divvy up de taxes.

CHRISTIAN: Uriah, how much dis island belongs to you, ye reckon?

ANAPEST: No more den sixty-five percent.

URIAH: Sixty-five! Eighty at leas'!

CASPER: Fader…

URIAH: Dese buggers tryin' to cut me short.

ANAPEST: Alright, have it your way. Eighty percent belongs to Uriah.

CHRISTIAN: 'Cordin' to reg'lations, dat means you pay eighty percent o' de taxes.

URIAH: What?

CHRISTIAN: Res' divvy up 'twix David an' Anapest.

ANAPEST: Now youse got to pick a teacher. Tell 'em who yur choosin', boy.

CHRISTIAN: Uh? I chooses Miss Mary Dougherty, from—

ANAPEST: Mary Dauphiny, boy, Mary Dauphiny!

CHRISTIAN: I chooses Miss Mary Dauphiny, from Bay o' God's Mercy.

JOSEPH: Mary Dauphiny?

DAVID: Picked 'er already, has ye?

URIAH: Anapest picked 'er, more like.

MELCHER: She one o' dem French gals?

DAVID: Cain't jus' take de firs' teacher comes along, Christian.

JOSEPH: We's got to make inquiries.

DAVID: Meet de gal, make sure she knows what she's talkin'.

MELCHER: Dauphiny sounds kind o' French, don't it?

CASPER: What kind o' qualifications dis teacher got?

ANAPEST: Ye kin ask 'er yurself. *(Yelling.)* Mary, git yur arse in here!

MARY DAUPHINY, a woman in her twenties, enters. She's more cheerful, less weather-beaten than the Rockbounders. She wears a red stocking cap with a tassel. The men gape.

MEN: **Hmm, hmm, ahh**

Hmm, hmm, ahh

Hmm...

MARY: Good ebenin', ladies, an' my sincere t'anks fur invitin' me to yur lovely island.

ANAPEST, FANNY & ALMA: Ebenin', ma'am.

MARY: An' may I say good ebenin' to you as well, gennlemen.

MEN: **Hmm, hmm, ahh**

Hmm, hmm, ahh

Hmm...

ANAPEST: Sailed ober all by 'er lonesome, didn't ye, Mary?

MARY: Dat I did. Water was beautiful an' calm.

ANAPEST: *(To the men.)* Ain't dat somet'in?

MEN: **Hmm, hmm, ahh**

Hmm, hmm, ahh

Hmm...

FANNY: Beg yur pardon, Mary. Dese fellers ain't de sharpest peelers in de pantry.

ALMA: Dey was inquirin' arter yur qualifications.

MARY: Fair 'nuff. I went to de county academy down Liscomb an' took me B certificate.

ANAPEST: Wid credit!

MARY: Den I went to de normal school ober Minden an' got me teacher's licence.

ALMA: Ye don't say!

ANAPEST: She's de darter o' Rollie Dauphiny, ole frien' o' yurs, Ury, an' a good man. An' she plays de organ somet'in beautiful, don't ye, Mary?

MARY: I trus' me qualifications meet wid yur approval, gennlemen.

ANAPEST: Worry not, Mary, dey approves o' yur qualifications. Don't ye, fellers'

MEN: **Hmm, hmm, ahh**

Hmm, hmm, ahh

Hmm...

FANNY: Is dat all ye kin say? T'ickheads! Dis here meetin's ober. Time to go home.

Everyone begins to file out. DAVID quietly approaches MARY.

DAVID: Pardon, Miss? *(Pause...then louder:)* Miss?

MARY: Yes?

DAVID: Please' to meet ye. Me name's David Jung.

MARY: David Jung? You dat David Jung I heard 'bout back home? De one's been high-line fisherman o' Duren Bay dese las' two year?

DAVID: Ay, Miss, dat's me. Miss, I'se wonderin': Do ye t'ink a feller as old as I is could larn readin'?

MARY: 'Course ye could.

DAVID: How does ye start?

MARY Firs' ye have to larn de alphabet.

DAVID: De A, B, C's?

MARY: Dat's right. Ye kin borrow dis here primer if ye

like. *(She hands him a book.)* It's called *De Firs' Royal Reader.*

DAVID: T'ank ye, I'se'll take real good care of it.

MARY: *(Pointing to a page.)* Here's de letters. Ye'll have to copy 'em ober and ober till you know 'em all.

DAVID: Dey's a string o' dem, ain't it?

MARY: Twenny-six. Den, when ye've larned yur letters, ye kin begin wid some simple words. Look, dis here's yur name: *(MARY writes.)* David Jung. An'—what's de name o' yur boat?

DAVID: *De Phoebe.*

MARY: *(She writes again.) De Phoebe.*

DAVID: I gots a baby, ye see. Me li'l Ralph. Anapest's raisin' him fur me. Some day he'll be comin' to dis here school, an' I'd like to help him wid his writin'. Reckon I kin larn, do ye?

MARY: David, if you kin outfish 'em all, from Liscomb to Minden fur two years runnin, den take me word fur it, ye kin larn to read an' write.

Scene 2

Two months later. URIAH and CASPER in the fish house.

URIAH: Firs' off—she went to school, so she kin keep some books fur us. Dat'll keep you an' yur brudder from wranglin' so much at de end o' de season. Second—she's a stout lass an' kin lend a good hand wid de fish when we's pinched. T'ird—arter ye marry 'er, she kin keep right on teachin' school jus' de same, an' any tax money Christian Kraus collecks for her will come right back to us! An' she's a pretty t'ing to boot. Ye fancy 'er, don't ye?

CASPER: Ay, Fader, I does at dat.

URIAH: I seen dat David Jung walkin' wid, wily bugger. She's ober his house at leas' once a week.

CASPER: Swear I don't know why women bodders wid trash like him. Ain't good fur nuttin', cain't read nur write, owns naught but a wee scrap o' lan'.

URIAH: De lad outfishes ye an' yur brudder pretty near ebery day, ain't it?

CASPER: Ye neber seen dat mackerel I caught las' week, Fader! Close to a two pounder, she was!

URIAH: Now an' agin' eben a blin' squirrel finds an acorn.

CASPER: If I was de Lord God, I'd wipe dat David an' his frien' Gershom Born right off dis eart'. Birds of a fedder, drunken whoremasters, de bot' o' dem. Nuttin' would do my eyes so much good as to see *De Phoebe* drive straight inter de Bull, Davy goin' down wid!

URIAH: If ye wants dat Mary Dauphiny, Casper, dere's no time to was'e. Ye gots to show 'er yur a proper man. I neber let no oder feller stan' in my way when I was young.

CASPER: Women's different now'days, fader.

URIAH: Ahh, women's de same as dey eber was. Trouble is'now'days men like you's too much like women.

Scene 3

The next night. DAVID's house. Evening. A paraffin lamp lights the room. MARY is reading from the "First Royal. Reader." DAVID and FANNY listen attentively.

MARY: Jane An' De Li'l Bird. Chapter Six, page twenny-two.

FANNY turns to page twenty-two, helps DAVID find it in his book.

Jane had a bird dat she kep' in a cage

It was so tame dat it would come to be fed from her han'

Now an' den she would let it out

Dat bird would sit on top o' de cage an' fly aroun' de room

No one else fed de li'l bird but Jane

Not goin' too fas' now, am I?

FANNY: No. It's a nice story, ain't it?

DAVID: Gal loves 'er li'l bird.

FANNY: Ay, she does.

All three turn the page.

MARY: **One day 'er aunt sent Jane a box o' new toys**

She was so pleased wid dem

She played all day wid dem

Dat day Jane did not feed 'er bird

FANNY: Poor li'l feller's gonna git hungry.

All three turn the page again.

MARY **Nex' mornin' Sally paid a visit to Jane**

Dey foun' de box of toys

Dey played an' played an' played

Once more de poor li'l bird got no food

FANNY looks at DAVID. All three turn the page.

When she woke up on de very nex' day

Jane found dat—

FANNY: Hang on, hang on! Don't want to hear de res' o' dis chapter. Ain't goin' to work out fur dis here bird, Mary, I kin see dat comin'.

MARY: Alright. Turn de page, den, an' we'll skip to de new words we larned. See 'em down dere at de bottom?

Aunt, bird, cage...

DAVID & FANNY: **Aunt, bird, cage...**

MARY: **Tame, box, toys...**

DAVID & FANNY: **Tame, box, toys...**

MARY: **Top, fly, r—**

There's a knock on the door. CASPER peeks his head in. He's wearing his Sunday suit.

CASPER: Hello?

MARY: Oh, hello, Casper.

CASPER: Ebenin', Mary. T'ought I'd stop by, see whedder ye an' Fanny'd like to walk home wid.

MARY: It's dat late already?

CASPER: Near half pas' eight. Ebenin' Fanny, ebenin' Davy. Still workin' on Book One? Been a couple o' mont's, ain't it?

DAVID: What ye wearin' dem dandy clothes fur, Casper? Been to a fancy weddin'?

CASPER: Jus' takin' a li'l stroll, dat's all.

MARY: Well, s'pose we should finish up. 'Member to review dat list o' words we went over, an' next week we'll move on to Jane An' De See-saw.

CASPER: Oh, dat dere's a tough one, Davy. If ye needs any help, jus' give a shout. *(To MARY.)* Been readin' me whole life, ye know.

DAVID: T'anks, Casper, but I reckon youse too busy countin' an' recountin' yur money day an' night to find de time.

CASPER: P'r'aps I should send me li'l six-year-ole cousin ober to help ye. He's started readin' Book T'ree.

MARY: Now boys, be nice.

CASPER: Jus' havin' a li'l fun, Mary, dat's all. Ain't we, Davy?

DAVID: Name's David.

CASPER: I'se'll drop ye off at de ole loft house, Fanny, den Mary, ye an' I kin cross de stubble field ober Anapest's.

MARY: T'anks, but David's already offered to walk me home, Casper. P'r'aps Fanny'd 'preciate de company.

CASPER: Fanny? But—

FANNY: Hold on to yur pickle, Casper, I'se'll git ye home safe an' soun'.

FANNY takes CASPER by the arm and pulls him out the door. MARY and DAVID step outside.

MARY: Bay looks peaceful tonight.

DAVID: Ay. Kin ye see Barren Island light, Mary?

MARY: I kin see somet'in' glowin' sort o' amber coloured, ober dere, by de point.

DAVID: No, reckon dat's some kind o' wessel, prob'ly one o' dem European trawlers. Barren Island's jus' to de lef'. Keep yur eye on 'er, she'll flash in a second.

(*Pause.*) Dere, see it?

MARY: Ay, David, t'ink I did.

DAVID: Frien' o' mine lives on dat island. Haven't seen him fur many a mont'. He'll be some surprised when he sees me readin'. (*He looks up.*) Bes' 'member yur umbrella on de way to school tomorrow, Mary. Mackerel sky, neber twenty-four hours dry. Don't want ye to catch cold.

MARY: (*She takes DAVID by the arm.*) Kin ye make out any constellations, David?

DAVID: Only one I know's de Big Dipper.

MARY: Larned 'em all when I got me certificate, ober Liscombe.

Dere's Orion:

Hunter of de winter night

King Poseidon's favourite son

No man, claimed he, could equal his skill

No woman alive could resist his will

Look, dere's Scorpius:

Sent one day to test Orion's stren'th

An' dough 'is spirit an' 'is bow were fierce

Dat scorpion's shell were jus' too strong to pierce

So Orion dove into de raging sea

MARY continues to gaze at the stars as DAVID sings.

DAVID: **She don't know**

When she points to de skies

An' she talks about God

An' she smiles wid 'er eyes

When she walks wid me home
An' we whisper good-bye
What she does to my heart
She don't know

MARY: **Now foreber dese enemies dwell in de heavens**
So to keep de skies peaceful de gods did decree:
As Scorpius rises each night to do battle
Orion mus' disappear into de sea

DAVID:	MARY:
She don't know	Poor Orion
When she points to de skies	Hunter of de winter night
An' she talks about God	King Poseidon's favourite son
An' she smiles wid 'er eyes	So proud, so bold
When she walks wid me home	An' yet, ebery night
An' we whisper good-bye	Orion's doomed to repeat 'is flight
But I know in my heart	Into de sea
I daren't say what I feel	Agin an' agin
It ain't right I should talk	An' agin
So it's all fur de bes'	
She don't know	

MARY: Nex' week we'll start readin' Homer, or p'r'aps Chaucer.

DAVID: Mary—

MARY: I know ye've only been readin' a few mont's, David, but I'm sure—

DAVID: I'se leavin', Mary.

MARY: Leavin'?

DAVID: I'se been asked to sail wid Johnny Westner, fishin' de Grand Banks.

MARY: How long will ye be gone?

DAVID: Couple o' mont's, a year. Could be longer.

MARY: Really. Well, it's... *(She takes his hand.)* It's an honour to be asked, David. Fader tole me de *Sylvia Westner* was high-line of de entire Liscomb fleet las' year.

DAVID: I'se sad at heart to be goin'. But my Tamar's only been dead a year an' a half, an' I'se still grievin' hard fur her. An' fur what I done. Mary, I ain't comin' back 'til I find some peace in me head.

MARY: *(Pulling her hand away.)* I unnerstan'.

DAVID: Will ye look in on me li'l Ralph ober Anapest's now an' agin while I'se gone?

MARY: Be glad to, David.

DAVID: I'se'll take me primer an' practice de words ebery day. Dat's a promise.

Scene 4

Two months later. The house of ROLLIE DAUPHINY, MARY's father, in Bay of God's Mercy. ROLLIE and URIAH are sitting by the wood stove, sipping hot rum.

URIAH: Real good o' ye to put me up fur de night, Rollie. Big rough out dere.

ROLLIE: T'ink nuttin' of it, Ury. I'se glad to take a draught o' rum wid. What ye sail in on?

URIAH: *De Lettie.*

ROLLIE: Still holdin' up, is she? Ye mus' o' had dat ole tub twenny year by now.

URIAH: Closer to twenny-five. Ye gots a new t'irty footer out dere, ain't ye?

ROLLIE: Ay. Got 'er from Boutilier. Needs a li'l work.

URIAH: Taken 'er out in de bay, has ye?

ROLLIE: Dat boat gits de wind behind 'er, she's like a gannet ridin' a wave, Ury. A goddamn gannet ridin' a wave.

URIAH: Ay, dats a nice lookin' wessel ye got yurself. *(They take a sip of rum.)* Dat gal o' yours, Rollie, I has to tell ye she's one hell of a schoolteacher, an' she's one fine lass.

ROLLIE: Dere's none like 'er on dis coast neider fur books nur work, an' she kin sail a boat, too, as good as air a one o' yur boys.

URIAH: Ye recall me eldes', Casper? He wants fur to marry yur gal if it kin be arranged betwixt us.

ROLLIE: Don't know if de lass'll take Casper, Ury. T'ink she's goin' 'bout wid anoder feller.

URIAH: It's dat David Jung, I lays. Ye tell 'er she cain't be t'inkin' on marryin' him, Rollie. He ain't got naught but a sliver o' land an' no gear to speak on.

ROLLIE: Lord sakes, it cain't be David, he's still grievin'. Ain't proper fur a lass to take up wid, an' I'd give 'er hell if she tried. 'Sides, David's been off to de Grand Banks dese las' two mont's.

URIAH: Well, jus' make certain ye remember, Rollie: Yur her fader, an' dat means youse de one got to choose de feller what's bes'. Young gals ain't got nair a lick o' good sense in dere pickin'.

ROLLIE: True 'nuff.

URIAH: An' ye know damn well'dey ain't a better match

up an' down dis here coas' den my boy Casper. He don't drink or carry on. He's got twelve t'ousand dollars in de bank. He'll be head o' de firm when I pass on, an' he'll inherit all me nets an' gear, an' ober half de land on de island.

ROLLIE: Ober half?

URIAH: He's me eldes', an' deares' to me heart he is.

ROLLIE: Hmmm?

URIAH: Casper's set on marryin' soon, Rollie. An' dey's plenny women count demselves damn lucky to git 'im.

ROLLIE: *(Pause.)* I'se'll talk wid Mary nex' week. She ain't goin' to like it much, but in de end she'll do as I tells 'er.

URIAH: I'm sure she will. Mary's a good lass. She'll see it's fur de bes'.

ROLLIE: Let's call it settled.

ROLLIE extends his hand. URIAH's hand remains at his side.

URIAH: Yur fergittin' 'bout dowry.

ROLLIE: Dowry?

URIAH: Tradition, ain't it?

ROLLIE: *(Pause.)* I'se'll give ye one o' me deep herrin' seines.

URIAH: Don't need no herrin' seine.

ROLLIE: Ten puncheons an' half a dozen trawl buoys.

URIAH: Got 'nuff puncheons an' trawl buoys.

ROLLIE: Well what are ye lookin' fur, Ury?

URIAH: T'inkin' p'r'aps dat t'irty footer ye got from Boutilier.

Pause. They stare each other down. Suddenly ROLLIE laughs out loud.

ROLLIE: Go ahead an' take 'er Uriah, yur jus' de same as ye eber was. But when ye repaints 'er, ye gots to name 'er "Mary."

Scene 5

One month later. CASPER and MARY are walking in ANAPEST's stubble field. There's a flag-pole in the field. MARY appears distracted.

CASPER: **Got me a fine new schooner, name** *Louise*

Forty-five footer, painted blacker den pitch

Wid a sharp strip o' scarlet 'long 'er scupper line from stem to stern

Ye kin see 'er copper bottom shinin'

Down below 'er bowsprit dey's a gilded figurehead

Looks jus' like a gal ober Liscomb name Louise

Feller who carved 'er went out grassin' wid Louise

Dat's how come

Wid bot' 'er top masts stepped

'Er yaller dories nested on deck

Jibs flappin' loose

De peak o' de mainsail hoisted up to dry

An' de breeze

Yawin' 'er to an' fro on 'er cable

She looks as supple as a seabird, she do

Bes' part is: Feller wanted two fifty
But I says, 'One seventy-five, take it or leave it,'
So de bugger takes it!
I would o' given 'im t'ree hunderd in a heartbeat
If he pushed
Stupid bugger

MARY: How's she feel on de open sea?

CASPER: Don't know, neber did care much fur sailin'. *(CASPER notices MARY looking towards the bay.)* What ye lookin' at, Mary?

MARY: Hmm? Oh, I'm t'inkin' we may be gittin' some rain. Mackerel sky, neber twenty-four hours dry.

CASPER: Heard David Jung say dat. Been talkin' to him, has ye?

MARY: Not since he lef' back in de spring.

CASPER: *(Looks her in the eye.)* You sure 'bout dat, Mary?

MARY: 'Course I'm sure. What're ye sayin'?

CASPER: Nuttin'. Jus' wonderin', dat's all. Why don't ye come wid ober de cabbage fields. I'se'll show ye what I'se plannin' to fertilize fur nex' summer. Lookin' at doublin' me profits, easy.

MARY: T'anks, Casper, you go ahead. I got some school work to do fur tomorrow.

CASPER: *(Pointed.)* Tomorrow's Saturday, Mary. Dey ain't no school.

MARY: What? 'Course tomorrow's Saturday, Casper, but I...I'm startin' a new subjeck—geography—on Monday an' I wanna git a head start dis ebenin'.

CASPER: Suit yurself. Uh, Mary? *(CASPER reaches in his pocket.)* Dis here's a flower I picked fur ye.

MARY: Dat's very nice, Casper.

CASPER: Guess what I'se doin' tonight.

MARY: Couldn't tell ye.

CASPER: I'se goin' to Bay o' God's Mercy. *(CASPER smiles.)* Goin' to have a talk wid yur fader.

MARY: Me fader? Oh.

CASPER: *(Pause.)* Well? Good ebenin', Mary.

CASPER awkwardly hands her the flower.

MARY: Good ebenin', Casper.

CASPER exits. MARY watches till he's gone, turns and waves urgently in the other direction, toward the bay.

Come on up. Quick!

She turns and waves again. GERSHOM enters. He and MARY embrace.

GERSHOM: Lord ye look good, Mary. I'se been missin' ye somet'in' fierce.

MARY: I was afeerd you wouldn't come, Gershom. Water's so rough.

GERSHOM: Wouldn't miss my Friday wid you fur de worl'. All I t'ink 'bout de whole week t'rough.

MARY: Me too.

GERSHOM: Seen ye talkin' wid Casper agin'. How kin ye put up wid dat weasel?

MARY: Fader says I have to give him a chance. Says he's a good man.

GERSHOM: A good man? A rich one, more like. Cain't stand to t'ink o' you walkin' 'round wid such a craven. Feller likes tillin' de soil better 'n fishin', won't go out on de water if dey's a li'l cloud in de sky! T'inks 'bout naught but his cashbox, dat one!

MARY: Casper walks home wid me ebery day after school, ye know dat, Gershom. What's wrong wid ye today?

GERSHOM: **Could be my eatin' too much corned mackerel**

Could be my fergittin' dat mornin' draught o' rum

But dey's a feelin' in me heart like a skipjack sinkin'

An' dey's a nip in de air says winter's soon to come

I know each an' ebery cranny from de Grampus to de Bull

I kin weave my wessel where de devil won't go

Jus' give me one quick gander at de land or at de sky

'Cause I'se a blind man come fog or snow

I kin haul on a halliard till de durn t'ing snaps

Let de tide rise up, let de Nort' wind blow

I don't give a sweet damn fur de t'under or de rain

But I'se a blind man come fog or snow

Won't set no sail

Won't ketch no herrin'

Cain't see no landmark

Cain't git no bearin'

Won't git no peace
Till winter's t'rough
Won't git no sleep
Won't come to you

Well, I kin knock off de hat o' any man on de Main
I kin jig on de fiddle wid me horsehair bow
I kin tell ye a tale make yur blood run cold
But I'se a blind man come fog or snow

Arter de snow hits, Mary, den de mist, den likely de ice clogs up de bay. I'd drive a boat t'rough hell fur ye, but soon enough dere'll be days an' whole mont's, p'r'aps, when I cain't git off dat island. An' ye'll have a nair a soul but Casper Jung to keep ye company. *(Pause.)* Marry me an' come wid.

MARY: Gershom, it's only been a mont' an' a half!

GERSHOM: Ye likes me, don't ye?

MARY: 'Course I likes ye, but…

GERSHOM: But what?

MARY: Yur jus' so wild and reckless at times.

GERSHOM: If ye'll have me, I'se'll change all dat an' be quiet as a woolly lamb, Mary.

MARY: An' ye drink rum like it's rainwater, Gershom.

GERSHOM: I'se'll stop dat too when we's married, I swear. Don't need de stuff.

MARY: Yur serious 'bout dis.

GERSHOM: Dat I is, Mary.

MARY: What 'bout skinny Molly Biddle ober Jenny Runover's?

GERSHOM: Come wid, an' I'se'll gladly say farewell to Jenny's gals fureber.

MARY: Uriah tole me he saw ye crouched down in yur kitchen, talkin' to some kind o' spirit.

GERSHOM: I talks wid meself, dat's true, got no one else to talk wid out dere. But don't listen to his chatter. I loves ye, Mary.

MARY: I know ye do, Gersh.

GERSHOM: Time's comin' fur ye to git married, an' yur fader's goin' to be tightenin' de rope 'round yur neck all winter, pushin' ye to marry dat Casper. Gittin' to ye already, ain't he?

MARY: Man's like a dog wid a bone.

GERSHOM: Now's de time fur us to do it, 'fore de ice hits! So—will ye have me or no?

MARY: *(Pause.)* I don't know, Gershom. Fader says I'd be safe wid Casper. He's got twelve t'ousand dollars in de bank. I—

GERSHOM: I gits eighty dollars a mont' fur keepin' de light, an' nex' summer I'se'll set t'ree halibut trawls an' mackerel an' herrin' nets. I'se'll work dese hands off fur ye, Mary, ye know?

MARY: Gershom! I can't marry ye now. It's too fas'. Unnerstan'?

GERSHOM: *(Pause.)* Alright, look here: you wait fur me dis winter an' I'se'll make ye dis promise: I won't go widin five mile o' Jenny Run-over's, an' I won't take nair a drink o' rum neider.

MARY: How kin I know ye're keepin' dis promise, Gershom? De winters are long.

GERSHOM looks at the flag pole.

GERSHOM: **When de snow starts to fallin'**
An' de ice settles in
An' I'se feelin' right lonesome
'Cause I bin t'inkin' on you

Ebery day I'se'll send ye a signal
Ebery day I'se'll fly a red flag
Cast yur eyes ober toward my island
An' den ye'll know dat I'se true

MARY: **When de snow starts fallin'**
An' de ice settles in
An' I'm tired of me fader
An' I'm tired of de childer
An' I long to hear you sing

Den let yur eyes slowly drif' toward Rockbound
An' if ye see my flag
I'll be makin' ye dis promise:
We'll be married in de spring

MEN:	WOMEN:
When de snow starts to fallin'	When de snow starts fallin'
An' de ice settles in	An' de ice settles in
An' I'se feelin' right lonesome	An' I'm tired of me fader
'Cause I bin t'inkin' on you	An' I'm tired of de childer
	An' I long to hear you sing
Ebery day I'se'll send ye a signal	Den let yur eyes slowly drif' toward
	Rockbound
Ebery day I'se'll fly a red flag	An' if ye see my flag

Cast yur eyes ober toward my island	**I'll be makin' ye dis promise:**
An' den ye'll know dat I'se true	**We'll be married in de spring**

Scene 6–Part 1

Two weeks later. DAVID and GERSHOM at Barren Island. DAVID's arm is in a sling. GERSHOM is raising a red flag.

DAVID: Youse a lucky man, Gershom. Dat's fur sure.

GERSHOM: Didn't expeck to come home an' find me gittin' hitched, did ye?

DAVID: No, didn't see dat comin'.

GERSHOM: Didn't see it comin' meself. But dat Mary Dauphiny's somet'in special, ain't she?

DAVID: Ay, she is.

GERSHOM: Kripse, Davy, ye look like a beaten dog. Don't worry, gittin' married ain't goin' to change me none. Ye an' I'll still kick up a ruckus from time to time.

DAVID: It's jus' dis here arm o' mine, Gershom. Hurts like hell an' I cain't hardly lift 'er. Wisht I could be more help fur ye.

GERSHOM: Don't fret 'bout dat, now. You jus' git yurself better. Do some cookin' an' some talkin'. Help keep me mind off o' dat ole rum. I'se cravin' it hellish bad.

DAVID: Doctor wanted to ampeytate, but I wouldn't let 'im. Says p'r'aps nex' summer might be able to do some light pullin'. Says I ought to be happy I'se eben sittin' here talkin' to ye. Damn rope could o' finished me off, grip on 'er was dat fierce. But I'd like to be back at it. Man needs to work.

GERSHOM: Ain't no p'int worryin' 'bout dat. Cain't get back to Rockbound fur a few mont's anyhow. Too much ice.

DAVID: Seen me li'l Ralph while I'se gone? Mary tole me she'd look in, but... Don't s'pose now... *(Pause.)* Ralphie jus' started larnin' a couple o' words when I lef'. Cain't shut de bugger up now, I lays. He's prob'ly jawin' like a jackrabbit.

GERSHOM: Look, dere she be. Mary's flag shinin' bright green, jus' like she said!

DAVID: *(He doesn't look.)* Youse a lucky man, Gershom. A right lucky man.

Scene 6–Part 2

MARY and ANAPEST are in the stubble field. MARY's raising her green flag.

ANAPEST: Gershom? Gershom Born? Has ye tole yur fader? *(Pause.)* Didn't t'ink so. 'Cause ye know what he'd be sayin': 'Ye want to spend yur life on a lonely island wid dat reckless drunkard? No trees, no flowers, no nuttin'; jus' solid rock an' dem hellish screamin' careys?' Barren Island ain't no place fur a woman.

MARY: Poor man, all alone out dere. Only pleasure he has is a drink o' rum now an' agin, an' I've taken dat away. Wish't I could hear 'im play dat fiddle o' his, or tell me a tale.

ANAPEST: Sure, he's good fur a tale or a tune. But Gershom Born ain't no man fur a wife, Mary.

MARY: Me fader wants me to marry Casper!

ANAPEST: Well, ye know what I t'inks 'bout dem Jungs. But Casper is a safe feller. An' he reads de Bible. Parts of it, anyways. An' he'll be de richest man on dis island when his fader finally croaks. But mos' of all, lass, ye bes' t'ink a long while 'fore ye go agin' yur fader's will. It's a child's duty to obey de parent, mudder an' fader bot'. Ye knows dat full well.

MARY: Wish David were here. He's de only person on dis island I kin talk wid.

ANAPEST: David Jung's gone, gal. Ober eight mont's, ain't it?

MARY: Said he'd come back, Anapest. Jus' needed to find some peace, den he'd come home. Dat's what he tole me.

ANAPEST: Well don't hold yur breat'. A man tells ye dat, ye don't know if ye'll eber se 'im agin'.

MARY: Hope he's kept up wid his readin'. When he gits back, him an' I'll read some Shakespeare.

Scene 6–Part 3

In the light house. GERSHOM's pacing. DAVID's reading a newspaper.

GERSHOM: Shakespeare's fellers in 'is plays was always drinkin' an' carousin'. Drank as much as dey felt like. Seemed to git on all right. An' me fader used to say dat Byron an' Shelley an' lots o' great mens was hellions fur women. No one tried to stop dem or make dem keep no damn promise!

Tried writin' 'er a poem las' night, I did. But ain't nuttin' much rhymes wid Mary. 'Cept fairy an' hairy. Where's me pipe?

DAVID: Gershom, listen to dis: *(DAVID reads very slowly.)* 'On de tent' day o' October, nineteen hunderd an' t'irty, de *HMCS Skeena* was launched. She'll be servin' in de Royal Canadian Navy at Portsmout'.'

Dey's a picture right here. Damn t'ing mus' be ober four hunderd feet!

GERSHOM grabs DAVID's newspaper and throws it on the floor.

GERSHOM: Where's me damn pipe, I said!

DAVID: Look on de damn table! Krily kripse, Gershom!

GERSHOM grabs his pipe from the table, starts to fill it with tobacco.

GERSHOM: Already mended me nets, overhauled an' rehooked me tubs o' trawl, painted me boat, an' laid a new plank floor in me boat house. I'se shot ebery stinkin' duck I kin set me eyes on, an' de news in dat damn paper ye're readin's ober two mont's ole!

DAVID: Have a bite o' corned mackerel. Take yur mind off de rum.

GERSHOM: I ain't t'inkin' 'bout no rum! An' it don't help none you talkin' 'bout it! I'se t'inkin' 'bout dat bastard Casper Jung. He's prob'ly talkin' to Mary right now, smilin' an' needlin' 'er.

DAVID: All ye eber talk 'bout's Mary, Mary, Mary! Would ye shut up 'bout dat gal fur one bloody minute? Don't do ye no good, nur me neider!

GERSHOM: *(Pause.)* Yur right, Davy. Let's talk 'bout somet'in else.

DAVID: Try t'inkin' on dat light o' yurs, Gershom. I reckon while us's sittin' here, somewhere out dere's prob'ly a liner, or a Liscomb boat, laden wid salt. Or p'r'aps a Norwegian barque. De captain, he's lookin' dis way, sayin', 'Ay, dere's Barren Island, so dat mus' be Minden Rockbound. We'se 'bout ten miles off.' Jus' from lookin' at yur light here, Gershom.

GERSHOM: *(GERSHOM nods his head.)* Ay, dat Casper's a crafty bugger, jus' like his fader.

Scene 6–Part 4

MARY's at the flag pole in ANAPEST's stubble field, looking over the bay. URIAH is hidden, watching.

URIAH: What ye doin', lass? What ye lookin' out dere fur? A red flag out Barren Island? What fur?

MARY raises her green flag.

Gershom Born! He mus' be yur feller.

MARY finishes raising her flag and exits. URIAH sneaks up to the flag pole.

Well ye ain't gittin' 'er, Gershom, not if I kin help it. Casper, if ye wasn't such a sluggard, widout no gumption to speak on.

URIAH pulls the flag down.

I'se'll be back in de mornin', lass. Raise 'er back up de pole 'fore you ketch on, pull 'er back down agin' come afternoon.

Scene 6–Part 5

In the light house. GERSHOM turns away from the window.

GERSHOM: It still ain't dere! *(DAVID's sleeping on the couch. GERSHOM rushes over and shakes him awake.)* Does ye hear what I'se sayin'? De flag still ain't dere. Two weeks now'nuttin'! Somet'in's got to be wrong, Davy. She wouldn't break 'er word to me, would she?

DAVID: No, Gershom, I'se sure she would neber—

GERSHOM: P'r'aps dat Casper finally got to 'er wid his lyin' promises an' fancy smiles. Twelve t'ousand in de bank, Mary said. All women cares 'bout's money. If she's taken up wid him, dey'll bot' pay fur it, I swear!

DAVID: Gershom, dey's got to be a reason fur—

GERSHOM: An' you sure as hell ain't helpin' neider. Lyin' 'round all day while I does all o' de work!

GERSHOM picks up a cup, smashes it. Then he goes to the flag pole, pulls down the red flag.

As fur dis here pennant, I'se had a belly full. I won't be no fool, Mary Dauphiny. I'se finished!

Scene 6–Part 6

MARY and FANNY in ANAPEST's stubble field. MARY is holding her green flag, looking out to sea.

FANNY: It's been ober a fortnight, Mary. T'ought p'r'aps Gershom were sickly, but ebery night dat light's still flashin'. An' if he's got de stren'th to light de light, he's got de stren'th to fly de flag. If he was in some kind o' trouble he'd send up a smoke so de gub'ment ice breaker would come git 'im.

I'se afeerd dey's only one explanation, dear: Tiger don't change 'is stripes. No p'int tryin' to make 'im.

MARY: *(MARY gives her flag to FANNY.)* Fader'll be very happy.

Scene 6–Part 7

That evening. DAVID's alone in the light house. GERSHOM storms in.

GERSHOM: Lyin' doxy! Dat twelve t'ousand were jus' too temptin'. She had to be de rich man's wife, lord it ober de res' of us!

GERSHOM runs to the floor plank, pulls out a jug of rum and drinks deeply.

DAVID: What ye mean, Gershom? Gershom? Ye tellin' me she married Casper?

GERSHOM: Dem Jungs played some kind o' dirty trick somewhere, I can feel it in me gut. Mary said she'd wait till de bloody spring, damnit! *(He drinks again.)*

DAVID: No, I don't believe it. It ain't possible. Mary would neber marry dat?

GERSHOM: Dey was married on Sunday. Hadn't eben finished tyin' me boat up to Anapest's launch when up runs Christian Kraus. Tole me his own self.

GERSHOM finishes off his jug.

Here, Davy, have a draught. We'se got four mont's bloody drinkin' to make up fur tonight! *(GERSHOM tries to give a jug to DAVID.)* Take it, I tell ye!

DAVID: De sun's low on de Ragged Cliffs, Gershom. It's time fur to light de lamp.

GERSHOM: To hell wid dat lamp! Let de ships run on de rocks. An' all de mens on board dose ships'let dere bodies be smashed! *(GERSHOM drinks again.)*

DAVID: Ye cain't do dat, Gershom. Ye'd lose yur job, an' Uriah'd git it. Prob'ly give it to Joseph, or Casper.

GERSHOM: Youse prob'ly right. Dey'd steal me light from under me, jus' like de bastards stole my Mary!

GERSHOM starts another jug.

DAVID: Slow down a bit, Gershom. Dat stuff's mighty powerful.

GERSHOM: Damn right. I'se gittin' liquefied tonight, I is, an' I don't care who'Hold on, Davy'listen. Hear dat?

The voice of the BLACK AND YELLOW DOG is heard. It continues underneath the scene, growing in intensity.

BLACK AND YELLOW DOG: **O di ba da o di o sha flo**

O di ba da o di o sha flo

GERSHOM: De moon's wanin' tonight, I lays. *(GERSHOM crouches down in a corner.)*

DAVID: What ye doin'? Ye ain't listenin' fur dat black an' yaller dog agin, are ye?

GERSHOM: Hush up, Davy. Cain't hear.

DAVID: Come away, Gershom. Ain't nuttin' dere. An' youse got to light de ?

GERSHOM: Hush up, I said! Or I'se'll smash dis jug o'er yur bloody head!

DAVID sits. GERSHOM stays crouched down for some time, listening intently, drinking occasionally, getting more and more distressed.

BLACK AND YELLOW DOG: **O di ba da o di o sha flo**

O di ba da o di o sha flo

Finally, GERSHOM staggers to his feet.

GERSHOM: **Hellish beast! Leave me alone!**

The voice of the BLACK AND YELLOW DOG disappears.

DAVID: Ye all right, Gershom?

GERSHOM: *(Pause. Then, very quiet.)* Sure, jus' a li'l tired, dat's all. I'se goin' to light de lamp. Den I'se goin' to bed. Tomorrow's a new day. Dat's what dey say, ain't it?

DAVID: True 'nuff.

GERSHOM: Davy, anyt'ing happen to me, I'd like ye to take ober dis here lighthouse.

DAVID: Gershom, dey ain't nuttin' goin' to—

GERSHOM: Will ye promise to do dat fur me?

DAVID: Sure, Gershom. 'Course I will.

Scene 7

The next day. URIAH and CASPER are at URIAH's dock. GERSHOM and DAVID are tying up their boat. URIAH has his duck gun pointed at them. GERSHOM has a jug of rum.

URIAH: **Us folk 'round here**

Don't want trouble

No p'int is it?

No p'int a' tall

Casper married 'er fair an' square

It's all ober an' done fur now

'Fore de eyes o' man

'Fore de eyes o' de Lord

So ye kin turn right 'round
Git back whar ye came from

Us folk 'round here
Don't want trouble
Ain't it?

GERSHOM: **Ain't dis a pretty kettle o' fish?**
He t'inks dat I'se come wid
me fists up
Ain't dis a pretty kettle o' fish?
I ain't come here to fight
I'se come to say t'ank-ye

URIAH: What do ye mean, t'ank-ye?

GERSHOM: Neber was de type to git married, Uriah. Ye know dat. Cain't git along widout me rum, an' dese womens won't let ye drink none. Here, Casper, I brung ye a jug. Fur gettin' me off de hook. Weddin' present from me an' Davy.

URIAH: Didn't figure on eber seein' yur face 'round here agin' arter we heard 'bout you gittin' all tangled in Johnny Westner's ropes. I reckon ye mus' o' felt like a damn fool when he found ye.

DAVID: An' I reckon ye got yur lobster traps set up in me house already, ain't ye?

URIAH: No p'int lettin' dat house go to was'e, now, was dere?

URIAH keeps his gun pointed. GERSHOM holds out the jug to CASPER.

GERSHOM: Dis here's de good stuff, Casper. Go on, take it. If youse lucky, p'raps ye kin sneak a swig now an' agin' when Mary ain't lookin'.

CASPER: What ye doin'? Eberyone knows ye was right sweet on Mary.

GERSHOM: Hasn't I been sweet on jus' 'bout ebery lass from here to Liscomb one time or anudder? But I like me gals ober Jenny Run-ober's too much to git married. What would skinny Molly Biddle do widout me to give 'er de ole Swedish scratch?

GERSHOM laughs. CASPER takes the jug.

URIAH: Ye come all dis way to give Casper a jug o' rum? Don't make no sense.

GERSHOM: No, yur right dere, Uriah. De real reason I'm back is all dem herrin'.

URIAH: Herrin'?

GERSHOM: Ain't seen 'em? Dey's runnin' 'round de Rock, t'ick as e'er I'se seen, like dat summer two year ago. But dey's too many fur one man. An' David's arm still ain't much good. Ain't dat right, Davy?

DAVID: Ay, but—

GERSHOM: 'Sides I ain't got no herrin' seine.

URIAH: Runnin' 'round de Rock, ye say?

GERSHOM: Out pas' Sheer Net Cove.

CASPER: Mus' be why we ain't seen 'em.

GERSHOM: I'se offerin' a t'ree way divvy—you, me an' Casper, straight up.

URIAH: Casper an' me was figurin' on fixin' de launch today, where de ice gnawed 'er.

GERSHOM: Alright, Davy, let's go talk to Christian Kraus, see whedder he—

URIAH: Hold on. *(Pause.)* We'll take *De Mary*. Jus' got 'er off o' Rollie Dauphiny. Holds more 'n dat ole boat o' yurs. An' I'se bringin' me gun.

Scene 8

One hour later. GERSHOM, URIAH and CASPER are on The Mary. *GERSHOM's at the tiller. URIAH is clutching his duck gun. CASPER's been drinking.*

GERSHOM & CASPER: **Ole Dukie's boat is painted green—A-ha**

Ole Dukie's boat is painted green

She's de finest boat ye eber seen

A-ha, doodle I dey

CASPER: *(Takes a swig of rum.)* I'se right glad to see ye ain't holdin' no grudge 'bout Mary, Gershom.

GERSHOM: No p'int. Ye won 'er fair an' square. Ain't dat a fac', Uriah?

URIAH: Damn right.

CASPER: See, Fader? *(Slaps GERSHOM on the back.)* Ole Gershom here's as pleasant as a bucket o' chips.

GERSHOM & CASPER: **Ole Dukie he sailed down de shore…A-ha**

Ole Dukie he sailed down de shore

To catch some fish from Labrador

A-ha, doodle I dey

GERSHOM: Kin ye see me flag flyin' ober Barren Island, Casper? Fader's ole flag, it is.

CASPER: *(Looks across the bay.)* Talkin' 'bout dat blue an' yaller flag, are ye, Gershom?

URIAH: Ain't blue an' yaller, ye fool. Gershom flies a red flag. Don't ye?

GERSHOM: Used t'er.

GERSHOM & CASPER: **Ole Dukie he looked all around...A-ha**

Ole Dukie he looked all around

'Me wife is dead, de blinds is down!'

A-ha, doodle I dey

GERSHOM: Uriah, quick! Couple o' sea ducks! Big fat ones!

URIAH wheels around, shoots at the sea ducks, misses.

URIAH: Ahhh. Damn t'ings too fas'. *(URIAH puts down his empty gun.)*

GERSHOM & CASPER: **'Sure 'nuff,' says Dukie, 'I don't care'...A-ha**

'Sure 'nuff,' says Dukie, 'I don't care

Fur I'll git anudder wife in de fall o' de year!'

A-ha, doodle I dey

CASPER laughs. GERSHOM takes a long swig of rum, then jerks the tiller suddenly and violently. CASPER and URIAH stumble.

CASPER: Careful wid dat dere tiller, Gershom! He he he! Almos' dropped me jug!

URIAH: Whar ye turnin', ye damn fool? Sheer Net Cove's back de oder way.

CASPER: Hush, now, Fader. You ain't de one seen de herrin', Gershom is. An' he knows whar he's headed, don't ye, Gershom?

GERSHOM: Sure 'nuff do, Casper.

URIAH: Ain't neber seen no herrin' out in dese waters.

GERSHOM: So here we is, de t'ree of us, floatin' on *de Mary*. Boat's almos' as purty as de gal, ain't she, Casper?

URIAH: Sheer off, Gershom. Water's too rough.

CASPER: Naaah, de gal's better lookin'. More ballas' in 'er keel! He he he!

GERSHOM gives the tiller another sudden jerk.

URIAH: What de hell ye doin'? Sheer off quick, it ain't safe.

GERSHOM: Ay, Mary's a nice name fur a boat, Ury. Real nice name.

URIAH: Look out, man! We'se gettin' close de Bull!

CASPER: De Bull? Holy liftin'! Ye bes' turn 'round, Gershom!

CASPER approaches GERSHOM. GERSHOM pulls out a knife, holds the tiller hard.

GERSHOM: **Eber seen de Bull, Casper?**

Snorts wid bot' nostrils, he does

Sprays high as de sky

An' roars somet'in' hellish

When he breaks

CASPER: What de hell ye doin', Gershom? He looks crazy in 'is eyes, Fader! Pick up yur gun!

URIAH: It's empty, boy. Ye have to run 'im!

CASPER doesn't move.

GERSHOM: **Steer ober de Bull, Casper**

Dey ain't no use prayin'

URIAH: I said run de bastard!

GERSHOM: **Eben God up above**

Won't dare journey down to de Bull

URIAH: Useless coward, out o' my way!

URIAH shoves CASPER aside, rushes GERSHOM with a ballast rock in his hand. GERSHOM lets go of the tiller, stops URIAH. Everyone freezes. Two streams of spray shoot high into the air as The Mary *enters The Bull.*

The voice of the BLACK AND YELLOW DOG is heard.

BLACK AND YELLOW DOG: **Ye ain't neber goin' to git no peace**
Ye ain't neber goin' to eben dis score
Till ye see 'em bot' jiggin' to an' fro
On de bottom o' de ocean floor

O di ba da o di o sha flo
O di ba da o di o sha flo
O di ba da o di o sha flo
O di ba da o di o sha flo

Scene 9

Barren Island Lighthouse. DAVID slowly ascends toward the lamp, where The GHOST of GERSHOM waits.

GHOST of GERSHOM: **When I grow old, and deat' comes callin'**
Don't lay my body in no hearse

Don't let de gals start caterwaulin'
Fur dat'll only make t'ings worse

Don't let no preacher preach no sermon
Fur I know my soul is cursed

Jus' dig a hole close to de ocean
Den whoeber gits dere first

Slip a jug o' rum inside my coffin

DAVID: **Case I wakes up wid a hellish t'irst**

The GHOST of GERSHOM recedes as DAVID lights the lamp.

Scene 10

One year later. Barren Island. ANAPEST, CHRISTIAN and DAVID are in the lighthouse, sipping some hot tea.

ANAPEST: Neber seen dis island lookin' better, Davy. Youse cleaned 'er up good.

DAVID: Had some hired help. Too much fur one man.

CHRISTIAN: Nat Levy tole me he'd been workin' fur ye las' winter.

DAVID: Ay. Nat helped me plough de turf an' plant spruces arter me arm healed up.

ANAPEST: Potatoes an' cabbages in de kitchen garden, ain't it?

DAVID: Ay.

CHRISTIAN: Mus' o' bin some job gittin' rid o' dem screamin' careys an' dem hellish herrin' gulls.

DAVID: Buggers fought pretty hard. I'se hopin' p'r'aps one day robins or sandpipers might nest here. Keep me company.

ANAPEST: Hardly seems right to call it Barren Island no more.

DAVID: *(Pause.)* How's Joseph makin' out? Relishin' bein' de new king o' Rockbound, I reckon.

ANAPEST: Dat boy's got twice 'is fader's greed, an' only half 'is brains.

DAVID: S'pose his childer be fishin' in a few years.

CHRISTIAN: Ay, an' dey's always fightin' an' quarrelin' wid my gaffers. Same's Melcher an' me done wid Ury's boys.

DAVID: Cain't say I miss it much, Christian. Eben if it does git mighty lonesome 'round here at times. *(Pause.)* How's Mary doin' ober at de school?

ANAPEST: Mary? Oh, she's gittin' along. Sometimes see 'er on Sunday night fur dinner.

DAVID: Got a new feller, has she?

ANAPEST: No. No, no, no, no, no.

DAVID: Reckon dey's a big lineup o' fellers jus' chompin' at de bit, ain't it?

ANAPEST: Mary ain't been goin' out much dis las' year, David.

CHRISTIAN: Sticks mos'ly to 'er books an' de childer.

DAVID: But she's gittin' along, is she? Sometimes ye see 'er—

ANAPEST: —on Sunday night fur dinner, yuh.

DAVID: Aunt Anapest, will ye do somet'in fur me? Nex' time ye see Mary, tell 'er I'se readin' a book by dat Homer feller she tole me 'bout.

ANAPEST: Why should I tell 'er? Ye kin tell 'er yur own self.

(Yelling.) Mary, git yur arse in here!

MARY enters.

DAVID: Mary?

MARY: 'Twas such a lovely ebenin', David, t'ought we'd surprise ye and bring dinner.

ANAPEST: Den tomorrow, she's goin' to marry ye, an' start a fam'ly.

MARY: Anapest!

ANAPEST: I says to 'er las' night, 'Ain't it a shame fur to leave dat strong man alone on Barren Island an' him a-lovin' ye to deat', an' ye a stout lass wid no man an' nair a kid? Ain't dat a pretty kettle o' fish,' says I to her. An' in de end she sees de p'int.

DAVID: Would ye really come out here an' have me, Mary?

ANAPEST: 'Course she would. She talks 'bout ye all de time, don't ye lass?

MARY: Not all de time, Anapest, but—

ANAPEST: Pretty near bores us to tears ebery Sunday, Christian, don't she?

CHRISTIAN: Ay, dat's a fac'.

ANAPEST: 'Sides, David Jung, I'se too old to be cleanin' up arter dat wharf rat o' yurs. It's time li'l Ralph lived wid 'is fader. Ye know dat's de trut' now. An' ye loves de lass, don't ye?

DAVID: I always did love ye, Mary.

ANAPEST: Den it's settled. Christian, let's go. Us'll git Reverend Green ober Big Outpost, an' pick up li'l Ralph on de way back. Should be here mid-mornin'. Now be good, you two. I mean it.

ANAPEST and CHRISTIAN exit.

DAVID: Yur sure 'bout dis, Mary? Kin be a tough life out here. Jus' twix' us, now: Youse got to be ready. An' youse got to be certain.

MARY: **I don't know**

When I look to de sky

If de rain's gonna fall

I don't know if de waves are too high

I don't even know who'll sail home

As I'm standin' dere wavin' good-bye

But what lives in my heart

Dis I know

DAVID: **Surely now a breaker's goin' to crash from de sea**

Sweepin' you, an' dis here light an all o' my joy away in its' undertow

Leavin' nuttin' but gravel an' beach rock

No? Den surely dis is some kind o' trick o' de Gods

Like in dat Homer book I'se readin'

Is you really a siren, or a mermaid?

No?

But surely I'se'll wake up, Lord, tomorrow

To find dat burden o' weariness rollin' back onto my shoulders

Eberyt'ing stolen away again

No?

Oh moon dat shines down on de sea

Is dat yur light pourin' down on me?

DAVID and MARY come together.

DAVID &
MARY: **Yes, dat moon dat shines down on de sea**
I feel its light pourin' down on me
I feel its light pourin' down
I feel its light pourin' down
I feel its light pourin' down
On me

The End.